Before You Marry

Before You Marry

Marry

Written Especially for Men

By
Clarence Nida

MOODY PRESS
CHICAGO

Library of Congress Cataloging in Publication Data

Nida, Clarence.
  Before you marry

  1. Marriage.
BV835.N53   248'.842   77-24175
ISBN 0-8024-0481-2

Second Printing, 1978

Printed in the United States of America

TO YOU, MY SON

Contents

Preface

It is relatively easy to counsel someone of the church family about marriage. The years of experience, coupled with the wisdom of others, have taught the counselor what to say and even how to say it. As a pastor-counselor, it is possible calmly to dispense the truths and, after the hours of discussion, feel personally satisfied and hopeful about the success of the marriage.

It can be a vastly different ball game when it is your own son who sits across the desk. Now I am a father-counselor, and the earnest young man is one whom I have loved more than life itself. He is the lad I sought to guide through the formative years, the teenager I watched mature into manhood. My heart, even a part of my life, is involved.

Other men's sons are also searching for help and needing answers to some large questions. Purely human wisdom, profound and informative as it may be, is not enough. There are invaluable scriptural principles and truths, but too often they are ignored and dismissed. Having sought to season my presentation with the salt of the Word, I hope the scope of the topics will reach to scores of keen young men who stand on the threshold of life's greatest and most serious adventure. There are so many imperatives that must be known, so many maxims to be laid down—to say nothing of the secrets to be shared—if the sweet mysteries of marriage are to be discovered in time. What is worth telling one must be worth sharing with others. Therefore, these words are for every son.

In a century in which more than a majority of marriages collapse and many others barely survive the turmoil of differences and the torture of conflict, may these words be used as a beam of light on the pathway of marriage. I hope these chapters will serve as a guide to all that God has to offer in this great venture of life to every son who contemplates marriage.

1

Special Girl, Special Needs

As you approach the day when you will say "I do,"
it is appropriate that a father share with a son some of
his knowledge garnered through the years. Any
young man needs added insight and enlightenment,
and this is particularly true for those who have been
denied the privilege of having a sister.

My first suggestion is that you need to know the
nature and needs of women. There are those who
question whether men will ever totally understand
women, for there is a difference deeper than appear-
ances. But the more you understand of their nature
and needs, the better will be your marriage.

Naturally, the girl in your heart is very special. The
Lord in His provident grace brought you two together.
She was brought into your heart and life to be a
helpmeet, companion, partner, and wife. She is
there to share not simply your love but your plans,
thoughts, and aspirations—every phase of your life.
Don't lock her out of any area. One woman told me, "I

was about to leave him." And the reason was simply that he had shut her out of his troubles, trying to shield her. A wife is meant to share in her husband's triumphs and sorrows, joys and disappointments. No one, except the Lord, can help in dark hours like an understanding and loving wife.

A woman needs a number of things in marriage. At the top of the list is the need for constant expressions of love. Many couples begin and close each day telling each other of their love. That is a worthy practice.

Women are "fearfully and wonderfully made" (Psalm 139:14), and their makeup requires generous amounts of empathy. Somewhere through the years, the inbred tenderness and sensitiveness are going to cause her to react in tears. To some men, tears are a symbol of weakness, a signal for battle, or even a weapon to force their surrender. Most men do not know how to cope with tears. One positive action is not to try to suppress or dismiss them. You must not walk away in despair or disgust. Usually there is a reason for the tears, so find out why! I discovered, after a few horrible blunders, that this is the time a woman needs comforting, reassuring love, a tender arm around her, and a shoulder to cry on. Above all, let her cry.

Either your wife will need an outlet for her own abilities, or she must become an integral part of your "team." You will do well to take delight in her successes. Her achievements must never be considered a challenge or a threat to your own position. It is a small man who cannot stand to see his wife succeed, even excel and reach the pinnacle of fame. God never intends that your wife fade into the background while you stand center stage in the floodlights.

The business world is so demanding of your time that a wife can feel neglected. Your wife must be made to feel essential to your work, for she *is* indispensable. It is a rare man who can be successful in the eyes of the Lord or man without a wife who stands beside him and strengthens his hand in God.

A woman thrives on sincere compliments. Needless to say, a score of areas call for them. Some men fail here because they are basically self-centered. Women need the approval of their husbands. Without it, beauty can wither and love fade. The true wife adorns herself in all her loveliness for her husband, and he needs to appreciate it. Let me suggest a few of the myriad of areas that merit compliments: dress, hair style, cooking, sewing. Naturally you will do well to praise her appearance. Tell her she's beautiful. Praise her achievements and always the meals. Remember, it is no small job to prepare and serve meals every day. You can think of a lot more, but the basic thing is to keep doing it. It isn't flattery; that's shallow. It is a loving compliment, and that will get you somewhere!

2

Ground Rules

Every marriage has its own ground rules, for no two marriages are run exactly the same. I have never found one that offers a perfect pattern. Not every standard fits every marriage because of the differing personalities of the partners. My advice for every young couple is: early in the marriage, work out your own rules, but be certain they do not violate the Bible's basic standards for matrimony.

Herein lies some of the challenge and excitement of the marriage. No one—no matter how brilliant, knowledgeable, or even maritally successful—can adequately advise you. With the wisdom the Lord gives to each of His children, and with His help, you can work it out! Just be sure that you both determine how you want to run your marriage and that you both agree to the rules.

Some girls want the total care of the house. Usually this is a good thing, for a five-thumbed husband certainly isn't much help. Other girls feel the kitchen is their domain and will only permit the husband to lift a lid to whet his appetite. One gracious and able housewife couldn't be bothered with her husband in the kitchen. She was all sufficiency. Furthermore, she felt he deserved the easy chair and the evening paper in those minutes before the meal. However, in a few homes the husband is the chef. It is not really a case of spoiling the wife; the couple just likes it that way. Some like to do the cooking together because it gives more time for companionship. Of course, it also means sharing some of the routine chores—"the drudgery," as some might express it.

Some women want to shop alone, asking only for the husband's cash or credit cards. Seeing some women's attire, it is obvious they need real help—the help a caring husband could give. Most of the men I have seen are obviously "dragged along" on shopping tours and look as happy as though they were attending a wake.

There are couples who agree that he should have time with the "boys" and she with the "girls." A few wives don't seem to mind being a golf widow. One of my friends overcame the problem by always taking his wife out after his afternoon on the golf course. It was something she looked forward to, and it alleviated her loneliness. One man tried to plan his golf game when his wife was going to be involved in another activity. But all couples need to have a time for recreation together.

The failure of many marriages is due to a lack of

togetherness. I believe the more things a couple can do together and enjoy, the happier and more successful will be their marriage. It is a sign of trouble when a partner feels the need to be apart or alone a great deal of the time. Some expound this concept: "The closer the objects, the more friction, so don't stay too close too long at a time." Actually, friction proves only that there isn't enough oil. When you really are in love, closeness is what you want! Most successful marriages differ greatly in the way they have been worked out. They have to fit the mode of living or life-style and the personalities of the partners. I know of two homes that are as different as can be, yet the women in those homes are sisters. Each couple has found satisfaction and contentment in their own arrangements. What I am driving at is this: Decide for yourselves. If the Lord can honor it and it is right for you, do it!

3

The Green-Eyed Monster

Marriage is a relationship of amazing strength, particularly when it is imbedded, like the cypress trees of the California coast, in the rock. Our rock is Christ Jesus. I've seen marriages survive the shock of sorrows and extreme difficulties, and withstand tempest and storm, even the trauma of unfaithfulness. It may seem to be a paradox, but marriage is also a delicate thing. It can snap when you least expect it. But always there is a reason.

Nothing is as destructive as jealousy. There is amazing agreement on this point among professional counselors, the marital authorities as well as pastors. It is staggering to survey the damage that can be wrought by this green-eyed monster. Psychologists call jealousy a "protective emotion"—one that makes you a guardian over the relation upon which your security and happiness depend. There is agreement that the bases of jealousy are insecurity, the lack of ability to trust, the doubt of real love, and the sense of personal inadequacy. Its definition is not as important as its existence in a marriage. I can never minimize its danger, for I have talked with too many caught in its vicious grasp, seen its demolishing power, and witnessed the debris left in its wake.

Jealousy can turn a marriage so completely around that what was to have been a dream come true becomes an agonizing nightmare. I shared a number of hours with a man and saw what living under suspicion had done to him and his marriage. I witnessed the irritation and resentment that spilled out. I also have the vivid mental picture of a young, loving wife telling me through her tears of the utter failure of her marriage. The bonds of love were severed; hopes and plans were shattered. She had given up because it was impossible to live with insinuation and accusations. I did not want to believe that jealousy could create an atmosphere that encourages the act suspected, but it happens too often to be doubted.

Ugly as jealousy is, one would think that man would bring it out into the open, assess its demonic power, and terminate its reign of terror. But instead, we excuse and justify it. The worst case I have ever seen was minimized with the suggestion, "Some people are just made that way." I've noticed that when it is so easily explained away, it is because that person has a case of the same disease.

Of course, some live under constant suspicion because they have been found guilty. A trust has been betrayed, and they have been found out. Apart from an infusion of divine grace, there is not much of a marriage left, despite the volume of promises and pleas for forgiveness, when there has been unfaithfulness.

Jealousy is hard to live with. The amazing thing about it is that it need not erupt; it can just silently and insidiously eat away at the heart of the marriage. However, given the slightest opportunity, it can run wild. No mate can handle this monster alone. It has more strength than a bear and more arms than an octopus, with which to ensnare its victim.

The life-style of our times, with its casual and careless displays of affection, can only foster jealousy. Here is another area where the Christian must move against the current. You must counter the trend with the determination that no act, look, or word could be misunderstood and incite jealousy. An ounce of prevention is worth more than a pound of explanations.

In the heart of each partner there is a natural possessiveness that emerged when love for each other first touched your lives. Each partner suddenly became protective of his love and loved one. This is a God-given emotion that acts as a guardian of the marriage. A wife would not be human if she did not react to a careless gesture, undue attention, or a provocative look. She knows that a spark can start a fire, a fire that to her means the beginning of grief and heartache. More than once a husband has been flattered by a word or look from someone of the opposite sex. His inadvertent or conscious response has caused his wife to be disheartened or upset.

A part of the solution is to honestly and openly face the problem. It will continue to burn in the heart unless it is brought out into the open and talked through with tenderness and understanding. To dismiss it as trivia is to scatter more seeds of jealously or to create a permanent disposition of jealousy. I believe that the chronic cases, those persons possessed by habitual jealousy, could have been spared the anguish if jealousy had been faced at its beginning. The answer is to work through the problem by discussing the feelings and the inner turmoil. Only then can the seething emotions that are tearing at the heart be dissolved. Then, with reassurances of love and by seeking the Lord's help in prayer, the marriage can emerge stronger.

One thing is certain: jealousy must be recognized as a foe. That is why it is imperative that it be dealt with in a spiritual manner. Real help ensues when it is evaluated in the light of Scripture. In Galatians 5:19-21 (NASB), it is listed in Paul's catalog of the "deeds of the flesh." In that light, there is no way it can be dignified. It is sin, plain and powerful! However, in that same passage is the guarantee of victory: "Walk in the Spirit, and ye shall not fulfil the lust [desires] of the flesh" (v. 16). Add to that promise the assurance of Romans 6:14, "Sin shall not have dominion over you." There is the marvelous provision of the cross of Christ to give confident victory. The indwelling power of the Holy Spirit can check and control jealousy. Whenever jealousy is at work, either silently or on a rampage, it is because the person is not willing to yield to the Spirit's power. The Holy Spirit can counter such a work of the flesh with the fruit of the Spirit.

My son, don't give this destructive demon even a chance to rear its ugly head. Deal with it by the power of the Holy Spirit, for Christ has made provision for victory. Do not let it shatter your precious trust. By no means allow it to bring clouds and storms into your marriage.

4

The Contagion of Moodiness

Some of the greatest lessons for living are taught in the classroom of personal contacts. Particularly is this true in the matter of moods as they affect a marriage.

I knew I was a fortunate man as far as marriage was concerned, but I did not realize how truly fortunate until I met a "Mary, Queen of Moods." She lived in her prison of gloom and moroseness. The effect upon her was bad enough, but what it did to her family should never happen, period! The one forgotten aspect in moodiness is that a mood, like bitterness, affects everyone touched by the moody one. This concept is confirmed by Hebrews 12:15, which warns, "Looking diligently . . . lest any root of bitterness springing up trouble you, and thereby many be defiled." This infection from his wife's bitterness explained the husband's twisted personality; his life was blanketed by despair.

Many marriages are infected by this chronic illness. It is not limited to a certain age or sex; it crops up as often in the young as in the aged. It is just as prevalent in the male as in the female, though the variety is usually different. (There is a vast difference between this prevalent malady of moodiness and the deep mental depression that many people suffer. The latter should be treated by a trained professional.)

There was a marriage I felt was sailing into a storm when I met the couple on their honeymoon. From the groom's actions and attitudes, you would have thought his world had collapsed. His mood was simply foul. I'm sure the bride was asking, "What have I gotten into?" You see, moods can emerge even on a honeymoon. They can and do surface at any time and place! That is why they are so devastating.

Moodiness is more prevalent than some might think. I was in a home once as a specially invited guest. The warmth of the fellowship was dramatically changed into frigid chill when the wife entered her domain as mad as a hornet. Naturally, the visit was ruined. I could not help but reflect that if she did not hesitate to discharge her poisonous mood in the presence of a visitor, what must she be like at other times? Out of this experience came a truth to be remembered: moods are destructive. I doubt whether my relationship with that couple can ever be the same again.

There are numerous moods. I suppose the spectrum goes from depression all the way to temper, with such intermediate categories as gloom, sulking, self-pity, weeping, and grouchiness. Nor do these moods complete the list, though they are the more pronounced and common. It is really disturbing when the guilty try to justify their moody meanness by pleading that it is innate, the product of heredity. Others honor their moods, suggesting they are a natural part of not feeling well. I knew one man who lived with constant pain, yet his joy was contagious. I have watched these moody ones defend their ways by suggesting that they are helpless victims, with no escape from the manacles of moods. Let me assure you that Christ, who "breaks the power of canceled sin" and "sets the prisoner free," is wonderfully able to deal with moods.

In defense of womanhood, there are times when for physical reasons, such as menstruation, some women cannot be their sweet, loving selves. Who could be emotionally calm and collected when the body is in turmoil? In addition, there is the possibility of a hormonal imbalance or a thyroid condition that can scuttle the emotional stability of a wife who has to struggle through the day. It is difficult to have it all under control when the body chemistry is changing. During these times a woman can hit the bottom, her emotions frayed. Things that usually can be handled with ease become sharp irritants. For the Christian wife, there is abundant grace for her needs. And a loving husband will learn to recognize the times and understand that they are seasons for extra love and exceeding patience.

Moods can cause wholesale havoc in a home. I have seen some husbands who even hesitated to go home because they were never sure of the mood of their partner. They never knew if they would get a kiss on the cheek or an emotional kick in the pants, some "sugar" or a shrug. They felt like tossing in their hat, and if that didn't come flying out, then they would venture in. A marriage is sweetened when you never have to wonder about your partner's mood. Then you can look forward to a loving reception, whether you are returning from work, the golf course, or the grocery store.

Someone has suggested that a partner needs to learn to read the mood of his mate and then roll with the punches. Personally, I find this a poor choice. Some persons would spend most of their time trying to adjust to the barometer of change. There are some obvious conclusions. No true Christian should excuse his or her bad moods, for these moods are the very thing that the Lord wants to eliminate from life. I have observed that when the new life in Christ begins to flow through a person, touching every area, the old, bad moods drop off. God's plan is to replace moodiness with His fruitfulness. One man, characterized by the phrase, "He has the most even disposition of any man in our community—always mad," was transformed into a radiant Christian, and the joy of the Lord filled his life. Christ is a Man of miracles!

It simply is not fair for a marriage partner to have to put up with moodiness. I have never been able to understand why some feel it is their privilege to take out their ugliness on the one they profess to love the most.

Beyond that, moods are a part of the sin life. I shall

never forget the wise words of one of my best friends. He rightly contends that there are sins of omission, sins of commission, and sins of disposition. There is no question but that moods fit this last category. Basically, moods are an element of the self-life. They indicate a state of carnality. The cross of Christ has made provision for moodiness to be dealt with in finality. A moody person has only to ask the Lord to help him to crucify the flesh with its affections and moods. Our all-sufficient Lord is able to handle it. Marriage is meant to bring happiness to your life. Don't let the contagion of moods infect what God wants you to have and enjoy.

5

Chivalry Is Not Dead

As you have noticed by now, many little things go into making a marriage dream come true. One of these little things is courtesy. Too often the gracious acts of courtesy go begging because the man who is courting has never been taught the basics. Some very brilliant and handsome males have woefully neglected this phase of their education. Otherwise well educated, they are totally uninformed about daily courtesies. The word translated "*goodness*" in Galatians 5:22 includes the idea of courtesy.

Some things are always right for the woman in your life. I am sure your parental instructions, plus knowledge gained from your experience and observation, have equipped you well in this area. I think that youth's rejection of many of the established practices of the past has not done away with common courtesies. Let me list a few rules, more or less as a refresher.

Stand up when a woman enters the room. Open the doors of a car, building, or home for her. Walk on the outside—the side nearest the road. These courtesies suggest you are her protector, and every girl who is a real lady loves that! At the table, help her to be seated. Help her with her coat. I may be challenged by the subway or bus commuter, but it is still nice to offer a seat to a lady.

I know a couple who are still very happily married after forty years. I have watched the husband sit back and with joy and pride listen to the repartee of his wife. Though she was not the most brilliant of conversationalists, to him everything she said was enjoyable and important. Any woman appreciates this kind of freedom and attention. So maxim number one is: let her speak! On the other hand, I've seen a woman give up in despair because of her husband's correction of insignificant details. Have you ever noticed the look of "when I get out of here, I'll—" on some woman's face when her eager-beaver husband keeps interrupting her with his wisdom and witticisms? It becomes obvious to all that anything she has to say is unimportant to him. What wife wants to be made to feel unimportant? It doesn't matter how brilliant the bit of wisdom you are bursting to share, it can wait until she has finished. Sometimes what we think "just must be said" is better left unsaid. Listening with courtesy to your wife might give you the time you need to evaluate what you are about to say.

Nothing is so fatal to marital bliss as the use of

28

someone else's living room to take a verbal whack at your wife. In the best marriages, the couple work out their problems in the privacy of their own home and at the right time. Timing can mean everything. It is all wrong for a husband to tease his wife or for a wife to belittle her husband in public. Often the remark becomes a blast that utterly destroys the other person. It doesn't take many such attacks to damage a marriage. No one—wife or husband—likes to be the object of laughter. Have you ever noticed that the best comedians laugh at themselves, not at others?

There are rewards for courtesy. It does something for your wife. It makes her glow within. There is a warm and loving response in her heart that never fails to pay great dividends. It always *says* something; it tells her, "You are very special to me." It says you care for her completely, not just for basic necessities, but in every area and way. These thoughtful gestures reaffirm your love. It is not enough to say "I love you." You must show it in sweet and simple ways, regardless of how long you live together. Show her the same courtesy that you did during courtship, the courtesy she is worthy of, and you will share a thousand joys.

6

"Stop the Marriage!"

"Stop the marriage! I want to get off!" Some are quick to say so. But do they really want out? It is easy to say, and certain circumstances can provoke the thought. In jest, a woman said, "No one has been married for any length of time who hasn't thought of murder or divorce." However, before you consolidate your thoughts into action, take time to realize what is really involved in such a decision.

Let's begin at the top of the list. When a couple contemplate the dissolution of their marriage, they need to look up! God is gravely concerned. Marriage is more than a contract made between a man and a woman and certified by means of a license. It is far more than a ceremony, civil or religious. No person should walk out of a marriage without thinking about the sacredness of the union in the sight of God. Whatever anyone does must be done with God in mind. Your decision does affect God. A young woman once shouted at me, "I don't care what God says" when she

30

was determined to terminate her marriage. Everyone had *better* care what God thinks! Each will face the Lord someday. Christians are challenged to please Him in all they do. When you stand before Him, will you be able to justify your decision?

Someone else is greatly involved: the girl you have taken into your heart and with whom you have made your home; the one you asked to be a part of your life. Just recently a mother told me through her tears how utterly broken was her daughter's heart. The wounds were so deep that she had wondered whether they could ever be healed. The one whom the girl had loved with all her heart, and to whom she had given herself completely, walked in and coldly said, "I can't be a father and husband." I saw her some months after she had picked up the pieces and after she had fought through the terrible heartache. The hurt of her heart was indelibly etched on her face and could be seen in her eyes. Her husband's action had made a terrible impact on this girl's life. What was done to her should not happen to anyone.

A pastor told me of his sister-in-law, who, after twenty-three years of marriage, plus the faithful nursing of her husband through three crucial illnesses, was stunned when he announced it was over. In this instance, as in most cases, there was another woman. This loving wife was plunged into the depths of despair, and her family wondered if she could survive the ordeal.

If only a man contemplating separation could see

these girls in the midst of their traumatic experience! He needs somehow to understand the agony, the deep wounds, and the bleeding hearts. When he walks out of a marriage, it is far more than an emotionless closing of a door. It is not as simple as turning the pages of the book of life to a new chapter. There are feelings involved, people with hearts that can be shattered, and dreams turned into an endless nightmare. Like it or not, you are a part of her life, and that can never be easily or totally changed. Memories can never be wholly erased. One man, who watched the suffering of his mother as she lived through the experience of divorce, said, "Mother never got over it. The love was there as long as she lived." Few women ever get over it! So think long and hard about what it will mean to your wife.

Many times the breakdown in the marriage takes place after children have been added to the home. The impressions on their lives are far deeper than most are willing to admit. Some of the children carry the scars through life and even into their own marriages. These little lives have a way of adjusting, but they are gravely affected. There is a great void in their hearts and a struggle to resolve the conflict of trying to love two sets of parents, if their parents remarry. They deserve far better. There is no way to minimize the effect upon the lives of children. They must be considered.

Then there is you, a part of this action. You may think you can hack it with ease. Don't be too sure. You have to live with memories, too—yours! And such memories are not turned off with a mere flick of a switch. When you want them least, they will come alive. It takes a lot more than you think to crush the emotions of your heart. Granted, some men are stony-hearted, but most of them are as emotionally oriented as women. You, too, can know loneliness, the feeling of an empty apartment, and the deep emotions of life. You cannot easily bury feelings like love and devotion. Although you may want to do so with all the fervency of your soul, these deep-seated emotions keep surfacing. Even if you are the initiator in the separation, it is not a simple matter. Search your heart carefully. Are you sure there isn't enough in your marriage to make it worth the effort of working out your differences?

About half of today's marriages begin with courtship but end in court. You are on your way there when you close the door on your marriage and open the door of an attorney's office. Usually the attorney is only interested in his fee. It is not your problem but your pocketbook that interests him. He is not seeking a solution to your difficulties, as minor as they may be, because all he can see is the dollar sign.

When you turn from heart-to-heart conversation with your wife, or reject the counsel of a marital counselor, in order to accept the guidance of the legal profession, you are facing the hard, cold judgment bar of man. You stand very near the point of no return. A dispassionate judge holds the destiny of your heart in his hands. No victory lies in the decision; rather, there is finality, if not brutality, in the transaction. The pounding of the judge's gavel after the decree can and usually does bang the door shut forever on your relationship with the one who once had an important place in your heart. You walk out empty and alone!

"I made a mistake" was the sad confession of one man who had wanted to bail out as a father and husband. No one can change the civil decision by wishing it away. By the time he had seen his error, it was too late. He had the rest of his life to live with the mistake. Now he knows that if he had thought it through, carefully weighing all that was involved and all it would mean to those affected, he would have found a way to make the marriage work.

You have to work at making a great marriage, but it is worth all the effort. Separation is no solution! Marriage can be wonderful—all the way from the beginning to end.

7

In the Mind of God

Think about the intentions of God in marriage. He is not to be an incidental factor. If a marriage is to be right, it will need to be "made in heaven"; "ordained of God," as the theologian would express it. God is vitally interested in bringing together two young lives. Our Lord is more concerned about the matching of the right man with the perfect maid than are the two young people in love. I have never understood why many Christian young people, who are willing to trust the Lord for salvation—their eternal destiny— and yield their lives in service wherever He leads, do not seek the Lord's guidance in pursuing a life partner. Actually, only God is really qualified to bring the one of His choosing into her or his life. Why not simply leave it in His able hands?

Consider what a fantastic job God did for Isaac. He had the right one, beautiful Rebecca, with a disposition of graciousness, in the right place, where she could prove the quality of her character, and at the right time. Moreover, God had made her heart ready to respond to the invitation. God knew that she would blend the loveliness of her life with the strength and sensitiveness of Isaac. It was love at first sight, because God had arranged the marriage. It was not chance; it was all Providence. If God could do such a magnificent work long before Calvary, surely He is not less able today.

The tragedy is that so few give Him the opportunity. It is all too apparent that today most young people feel eminently and solely qualified to find the right one. When you leave God out of the choosing, how can you expect His blessing in the living out of your marriage? It is wrong to make plans and then ask God for His benediction and beneficence.

When a marriage is contracted that runs counter to the directives of Scripture, it is courting everything from disappointment to disaster. An unequal yoke will rarely work. I can recall a score of unequal unions, marriages begun in spite of knowing the scriptural warnings. Their paths were strewn with the thorns of bitterness, regret, and heartache. Few blessings brightened the way. No one can violate the commands of the Word and still know God's favor.

Marriage is forever! This is both the decree and design of God. Without getting involved in a dialogue on divorce, and without posing as an authority with the last word on the subject, let me say that it is God's intention that the marriage is to last through all the years God grants to those two lives.

Many loving couples have a secret hope that there is a special togetherness for them in heaven. You cannot read the Scriptures without realizing that God intends marriage to be permanent. This is understandable when you consider the union that takes place. He cannot sanction the dissolution of such a sacred union. In the light of the divorce rate, I must emphasize strongly the foreverness that is in the mind of God. This should be the considered conviction of those who enter into a marriage. Although they may not admit it, far too many have the attitude that if it doesn't work, there is an easy way out. That may be the twentieth century view, but more often it is a myth, and certainly it is not God's manifest will.

There is another sublime yet simple truth: marriage is "forsaking all others and cleaving" to each other. It may sound easy, but it is truly difficult for some. You may not believe that you might have a problem here, because now you can't wait to cleave! You are counting the days until you "forsake father and mother" and begin to create a new home and identity.

But knowledgeable as you may be, it will not hurt to take some time to consider the particular "for this cause" that God cites in Scripture. Some have a hard time cutting the ties that bind! Girls are especially vulnerable in this area, owing to a deeper attachment to their parents and home. Love, understanding and the patience of Job, will go a long way toward helping your partner over this hurdle.

The marriage that lasts will put God first from the

opening chapter of courtship right on through the closing paragraphs of life. He will not just be present in their lives, but also preeminent. The Lord will be at the center as well as the circumference. This kind of marriage doesn't just last; it knows something about heaven on earth.

8

Making It a Great Marriage

A majority of marriages ramble on with neither rhyme nor reason. However, in the few that can be called great, there is both rhyme and reason, and the marriage becomes a beautiful poem. Before citing some of the basic reasons for their greatness, let me set forth a few general truths about great marriages.

First of all, they are not the result of happenstance; rather, they are the product of Providence. It is God at work in human lives, plus the determination and perseverance of the participants, that makes a great marriage. Second, great marriages are not dependent upon affluence, prestige, security, or fame. You will find them more often in homes that could be classified as "Be it ever so humble, there's no place like" it. Third, great marriages are not common. What passes in today's market as ideal is usually far from genuine greatness, because the pattern has been replaced and so the product is cheapened.

God in His grace probably allows every person to

view and be touched by a great marriage. Do not miss your opportunity to take a long look so that you can discover its secrets. When you evaluate the garnered information, several basic factors will be evident.

Those who achieve greatness in marriage do not use some easy formula, nor is the marriage programmed by a computer. They put something into it—namely, love. The partners are deeply in love and express it constantly and consistently. Their love is durable, able to withstand everything from disappointment to disagreement. Every marriage needs ardent love, for it sustains the joy and happiness you seek. Lasting love will carry you through the dark valleys. A superficial love, which has physical attraction as its basis, will carry a couple into some grim experiences, but never through them.

A second essential is dependency—a need for each other. In *The Further Adventures of Robinson Crusoe*, Daniel Defoe has Crusoe say, when reflecting on the loss of his wife:

> She was, in a few words, the stay of all my affairs, the center of all my enterprises and did more to guide my rambling genius than a mother's tears, a father's instructions, a friend's counsel, or all my own reasoning powers could do. I was happy in listening to her tears and in being moved by her entreaties, and to the last degree desolate and dislocated in the world by the loss of her. My sage counsellor was gone, I was like a ship without a pilot that could only run afore the wind.

40

In a marvelous way, these words speak of dependency.

I viewed a great marriage one day. As I sat at the table with my hosts, I watched the devotion of the wife, who, as she took his hand in hers, said, "He is my life." Every partner must be made to feel and know he or she is needed—indispensably. Call it partnership, interdependency, or just a sense of needing one another, yet it is basic if greatness is to be found.

Knowledge is another important factor in success. A marriage will not get off the ground if a man is ignorant of its nature and involvements. Marriage is not merely a convenient arrangement, a license for sex, an escape from loneliness, or a means of rescue from parental domination. It is a bit of heaven on earth, where love, fulfillment, companionship, and joy make life all that it is meant to be. Don't contemplate walking down that aisle until you know your role, the part you play in the drama. Unless you are truly knowledgeable, what should be romantic joy will turn into stark tragedy.

Every potential husband needs to know all he can about the nature of woman. She is an amazing creation! Her emotions, like a harp, are strung tightly and are just as responsive, numerous, and beautiful. Because she is very sensitive, she can become elated by a gentle touch or crushed by a harsh word or a look of disapproval. Her heartstrings are made of delicate fiber that can be impaired by coldness, indifference, or intemperate outbursts. When these inner chords are damaged, even slightly, they are difficult to restore.

A woman also has a deep inner strength that may surprise you. She can bear a score of burdens and cares, yet still give you all the love you can handle. She will go anywhere, accept any challenge, suffer hardships for you and with you if she knows you love her. You will never totally fathom all she is, so never underestimate the wonder of womanhood.

A dynamic faith is a large factor in a good marriage. There may be a few that excel without it, but they are the exception and not the rule. Faith in the Lord must be alive and personal, for real harmony and abiding happiness are dependent upon it. I have never seen a home that did not need God's daily blessing. Who else can blend the personalities, smooth out the rough places, soothe the spirit in the midst of differences, and solve the difficulties? Without the Lord, a marriage can only blunder through. Only the Lord can take the emotions, backgrounds, character traits, and personalities and weave them into a garment of strength and beauty.

Finally, mixed in with the other elements is confident determination. Recently a partner in a superior marriage said, "There were some real problems along the way, times of stress and hardships, but we never gave a thought to failure in our marriage. You have to work at it, and we were determined to make it work." A great marriage is possible, is worth more than all the work it requires, and is of greater value than the wealth of this world. Don't settle for less than greatness!

9

You Need Her!

When I suggest that you will need your wife, doubt-less your response is "Tell me something I don't know!" All right, I will. What you do not know is how much and in the variety of ways you will need her.

You are very much aware that you need her companionship. Not many men can make it alone, and God made us that way. The understatement of the year is that life would be awesomely lonely without the pleasant companionship of a charming and congenial wife. A happy relationship is built in part on the enjoyment and satisfaction of being together.

But God did not make women just for man's comfort and joy. A man also needs a woman's help over the humps and bumps of life. That is part of the helpmeet role. Most women can fulfill that role in a spectacular way, because they are especially endowed with the ability to challenge and cheer. A gracious word or loving embrace can turn the darkest night into a bright day. They seem to have a special talent for pulling a man from under the proverbial juniper tree.

Even though a man finds it hard to admit, he needs a wife to help him grow. For although he can grow a generous moustache and a heavy beard, there still remains a need for further maturing. It is a wise husband who will seek his wife's help in the improvement department. Doubtless some men never seek it because they fear a takeover, but they are the losers.

Even though you dislike the lecture method, don't refuse the help of an able wife. I knew a man who jested about the lectures his wife gave him, but he was a better man because of them.

When a wife's help is rejected, the problem is basically that the egotistical husband thinks he doesn't need help. Some men feel they are eminently qualified to make their own self-improvements. Whenever I see a man who boasts about being self-made, I am reminded of a little girl who, when she met such a man, looked him over very carefully and then said, "Why did you make yourself like that?" I have often thought that if a man were to allow his wife to work on the project, he would be spared many of the sharper instruments that God then has to use in the perfecting process.

A loving wife wants the best *for* her husband and wants to find the best *in* him. There are flaws and faults that a loving wife can help you correct, so you will do well to trust her skill and submit to her gentle touch. Her gracious corrections will be preferable to

45

the barbed instruments of some compassionless critic.

You need her wisdom, counsel, and criticism. Do not be shortsighted and refuse to seek them. Two heads are always better than one, particularly when the hearts of the two are united. Since a man does not have all the answers, you will do well to keep the lines of communication open in these areas as well as in family and marital discussions. Further, no man can be sure how he is being received, how he is "coming through" to his associates, but a good wife has the power to sense the situation and read their response. No one can help you in the areas of your needs better than a wise and winsome wife. I have seen a score of men who needed the help their wives tried to give them.

A man who can honestly express appreciation for his wife's suggestions will put a halo around his head as far as she is concerned. There is another plus in it, too: it will deepen her love for you.

You need her partnership in prayer. Remember the promise, "If two of you shall agree . . . as touching any thing that they shall ask, it shall be done for them of my Father" (Matthew 18:19). Nothing can knit together two hearts as strongly and deeply. Life has its burdens, but none of them are so great that they cannot be lifted when brought by two praying hearts to the Burden-Bearer. Every man's vocation has its difficulties. But these can be overcome in the strength of the Lord, which is derived as you pray together. Even

Christ wanted companionship in prayer as He faced the cross. A man who has a praying companion for any crisis is greatly blessed. In a wonderful way, God hears and answers when a husband and wife bow together at the throne of grace, where there is always help to be found in time of need.

10

The Marriage Manual

The Word of God is a great marriage manual that speaks lucidly about the inner workings of the marriage relationship. You can build a successful marriage on the foundation of just four things found there. I'm not suggesting that such a foundation is all that is needed, but it will go a long way toward establishing a beautiful and lasting marriage.

Incidentally, it is amazing how the apostles Paul, the bachelor, and Peter, the married man, agree on marriage. In my devotional reading, I notice that Peter takes time out in his message about suffering to give instructions on marriage (1 Peter 3:1-7). Basically he suggests respectfulness, faithfulness, and modesty for the wife.

Since I'm writing to you, the prospective husband, let me put more emphasis on your obligations. Peter has a great word for all of us men when he says to live considerately and also to give honor. It's a poor translation if you limit "giving honour" to mean courtesy.

Obviously, few men know of the existence of this verse. These two biblical imperatives should be accepted and practiced before you ever think about being the "head of the wife" (Ephesians 5:23).

In the days of courtship, a man is all consideration. A young man in love will utilize every opportunity to manifest thoughtfulness and kindness. Just one word of encouragement: keep it up! Let the acts of consideration continue through all the years the Lord gives you together. Many marriages crumble because the thoughtfulness and kindnesses of courtship cease soon after the vows are spoken. Never take your marriage for granted. The great marriages that I have observed have large amounts of considerateness in them.

A second part of the foundation must be to bestow honor. There is only one throne in your heart, and Christ is always to occupy that. Yet there is a place of honor, and the wife must remain there. As she stands there as a bride in all her splendor, let her gown be your protectiveness and her jeweled crown your expressions of love. Even though it is a second position, a loving Christian girl is content to have this wonderful place in your heart. This is not a directive from a dad, but the inspired plan of God. When this order is established and maintained—Christ first and the beloved in her place of honor—your marriage is promised God's blessing. I am convinced that God wants a marriage to be more than lasting. In His purpose it is to be a thing of beauty and a joy forever.

There is a good word directed to husbands in Paul's letter to the Ephesians. This is the phrase most men know and vehemently affirm: "The husband is the head of the wife" (Ephesians 5:23). It is the divine order. The secret of harmony in the home is found here. Most wives who walk with the Lord want their marriage to be lived in compliance to this directive, and they gladly yield the position of headship to the spiritually responsible husband who has captured their hearts. He is supposed to take charge. However, being the head means leadership, not lordship. Only Christ is the Lord of the home. Some marriages have become battlegrounds because the husband mistook leadership for dictatorship.

When you reflect on the headship of the husband, you must consider responsiveness as well as responsibleness. As the head always responds to the needs of the body, so the husband, assuming this God-given role, must respond quickly and graciously to the needs of his wife. I have counseled too many who felt that in order to lead they must dominate. That is not leadership! The Lord is not pleased with a domineering and demanding husband. How can the wife be the helpmeet God intended her to be if the husband crushes her personality, drives it behind a shell of fear, or causes her talents to shrivel? Some husbands have twisted submission into sublimation, where the wife loses her identity and her personality is stifled. This makes the home a prison and the relationship one of bondage.

Paul speaks of the primacy of love when he says that there "abide faith, hope, and love, . . . but the greatest of these is love" (1 Corinthians 13:13, NASB). The greatest element of marriage is true love. Love will regulate leadership and make it both sensible and sensitive. Love will blend leadership with consideration. Love will make the gears of the marriage relationship mesh so that it will be both attractive and productive. And remember that your love is to be the kind that Christ has for the Church. You can hang this verse on your heart: "Husbands, love your wives, even as Christ loved the church" (Ephesians 5:25)." You can't love your wife too much, for a woman responds to love and needs large daily doses. Love can either grow or die. When two hearts are brought together by the Lord, love can only increase, with the seal of His blessing.

The biggest three little words in marriage are, of course, "I love you!" Ballads have been sung, poems written, and love stories related by the score; yet none have done the subject justice. Love is the main issue! Love is the theme. It is the warp and woof of every marriage.

No one has ever adequately answered the question, "What is love?" I have asked every couple who sought my help for either marriage counseling or the performance of the marriage ceremony to tell me the nature of love. About all they could answer was "You just know when you've got it or it has got you." That is not an adequate answer, and doubtless its inadequacy explains the reason for the failure of so many marriages.

How do you really know when you are in love? There comes that decisive moment in your life when suddenly *she* is in your heart, your mind, and, you might say, your soul. One thing is certain: you become alive unto her. It is her face, her eyes, her voice, her presence that fill your mind and thrill your heart. It isn't a girl or even some girl you long to be with; it is that particular face you want to see and her voice you want to hear. She is *the* girl in your life!

Your every plan for all your tomorrows has her in it. You cannot envision life without her. You want to be with her every moment and share every experience. You can freely bare your heart to her. Positively, emphatically, you *are* in love!

This is not to be confused with momentary infatuation with a face, the loveliness of a lady, or a fun person. Nor is it to be classified as physical attraction. Promiscuous petting and excessive necking distort the understanding as they play havoc with the heartstrings, for then it becomes impossible to distinguish between real love and a fleeting flirtation. Love is not a condition, like the measles, that shows when you have it. True love demands expression; it can never be contained. It is bound to surface and burst forth. I have seen a seed, buried in a cleft of a rock, rise to beauty and strength until the rock was broken. Your love should be like that, thrusting its way through to expression. The brilliant poetess Elizabeth Barrett

Browning put it in a sonnet: "How do I love thee? Let me count the ways." If you take this out of poetry and put it into life, it might be better said, "Let me show you the ways I love you." Any young man worthy of another's love will find a myriad of ways. Love will find the right words to say, but do not let it stop there. Be sure it is evident in your attitudes, feelings, and actions.

A wise person once said, "We are never more like God than when we forgive." The same could be said of ardent love, for God is love! Of course there is a difference between divine love (Greek, *agape*) and the love you have for the girl of your dreams. In a Christian's life, the divine love will blend with human love, fortifying it. The "more excellent way" described in 1 Corinthians 13 is not meant to be purely academic. It is to be expressed in life. The interweaving of human and divine love will give your marriage unique strength and beauty.

Furthermore, here is the standard, in capsule, for your love: "Love is patient, love is kind, and is not jealous; love does not brag and is not arrogant, does not act unbecomingly; it does not seek its own, is not provoked, does not take into account a wrong . . . bears all things, . . . endures all things . . . never fails" (1 Corinthians 13:4-7, NASB). This can challenge you for a lifetime.

In real love there is also a giving element. It may well be the central factor. This is a truth unfolded in the Scriptures. "God so loved . . . that He gave" (John

3:16, NASB), and "Herein is love . . . that . . . God . . . loved us, and sent his Son to be the propitiation [sacrifice] for our sins" (1 John 4:10). Genuine love, divine or human, will cause the one who loves to give of himself. Love can never be exhausted, so be sure to give it lavishly. The love that makes the marriage is the kind that prompts you to give yourself totally to and for your partner.

I really don't know anyone who is an authority on love, unless it is someone who has never been in love. Yet this I know: each must give of himself to make the marriage all that it can be. Many marriages break down right here—in giving love. Too many are willing to receive all the other has to give, but are unwilling to be the giver. Remember, my son, the male has a terrible tendency to love himself while failing miserably in giving his love.

All of us need love, some more than others. Most of us have a tremendous capacity to love. A wise husband pours forth love out of his abundant treasury. The successful husband never lets a day go by without expressing his love. No wife should ever have to wonder for a moment about being loved solely and totally.

True love is unchanging. With the passing of the years, it should deepen and increase. Change and decay may be seen in many things, but not in love that is blessed and sustained by the Lord. I have seen love endure in the lives of friends and loved ones through the crises of sickness, heartbreak, and physical hand-

54

icap. These couples not only took seriously the vow "for better for worse, for richer for poorer, in sickness and in health, to love and to cherish," but they also possessed a love that would not change.

Another factor of love is that it thrives best when there is response. Actually, it cannot survive without response. For love to blossom in all its beauty, it must feel and know love in return. It takes interaction of heart with heart, shared tenderly and generously.

Two young lives with the faculty to give and receive love are in for some wonderful experiences through all the years of their marriage.

11

"Happily Ever After"

Success in marriage is not automatic, even if you are a Christian couple. You must work at it! Therefore, it is imperative that you know what marriage really is.

First and foremost, marriage is a divinely ordained relationship. "For this cause shall a man leave ... and shall cleave" (Matthew 19:5) goes back to the beginning of man's sojourn upon the earth. Contrary to the tenets of the new morality, brazenly expressed and exhibited by its advocates, marriage is not a matter of choice, as if two can live together without it. It is not a simple part of the structure of the establishment that can be assaulted and destroyed.

In the mind of God, marriage was authorized for the continuation of life upon the earth. The divine command was, "Multiply, and replenish the earth" (Genesis 1:28). God provided a wonderful gift so that His procreative purposes could be fulfilled by mankind. Marriage is not merely a convenient arrangement to satisfy man's sexual appetite. It is God's way for two to live together, to express their love totally, and to find complete fulfillment in love.

The words "It is not good for the man to be alone" (Genesis 2:18, NASB) suggest that man is incomplete by himself. The marital union is a fusion of two lives and two personalities so that each is complete with the other. Completeness, in a marvelous and almost mystical way, is found when two "become one flesh" (Genesis 2:24, NASB).

Originally, marriage was instituted of God so that eternal truths, divine promises, and covenant relationships might be transmitted from one age to another. This is almost a forgotten purpose in marriage.

As one marriage ceremony states, "It is an institution of God, ordained in the time of man's innocency, before he had sinned against his maker and been banished from paradise. It was given in wisdom and in kindness." Marriage is of God and is therefore sacred and holy.

Marriage is a union. It is meant to be total. The physical union takes place with the first act of love and continues and increases until death parts the two. It is the blending of two hearts and lives as well as two bodies. One great man of God said, "Marriage is a soul wedded to a soul, so that they become twin souls." Here is deepest intimacy. The more complete the union, the more beautiful and rewarding the marriage.

Marriage is creation, the creation of a new entity: a family. As such, it is a dynamic thing moving toward either maturity or disintegration. It is like life itself. A man said to a friend, "You're surely getting older." The man replied, "I like that better than the alternative." Likewise, marriage either grows or decays. Observation of the best marriages is instructive, for we learn that it is not only meant to grow, but that it *can*. Again, like life, it must be nurtured and cared for. Every marriage has the capacity for growth, but all too few are supplied with the nutriments of affection, consideration, devotion, and spiritual practices.

Marriage is a partnership. It is meant to be a merger, not a takeover. It is an equal blending, a joint venture made possible by the equal deposits of emotion and character by both husband and wife. Each has a zone of responsibility, a sphere of influence, but there is an interdependency, a sharing of goals and gains, duties and destiny. One thing that should be boldly established, and to which the partners should give complete assent, is that there is no place for a feeling of superiority, an "I'm better than you" attitude. Nothing can mar a marriage partnership faster. Some things only she can do and do well. Try giving birth to a child or being a mother. No matter how competent a man may be, a true home cannot exist without a mother. Husbands and wives are meant to complement one another.

Marriage is companionship. *Sharing* is an essential word in marriage, a word that everyone can understand. There must be sharing of experiences, varied as they may be. There must be companionship in accomplishments or failures, sorrows or successes. One element of companionship is often ignored— that of sharing of the mind. Few marriages have an interchange of thoughts. Every wife wants to know what her man is thinking, because she wants to be a part of *all* his life. But some men never bare their thoughts, and their periods of silence, coupled with a faraway look, can build unnecessary barriers. Sharing your thoughts with your partner can be both helpful and stimulating, for a woman has valuable intuitive knowledge. More than one husband has been grateful for the wealth of information garnered through the years from his wife's mental treasury, a treasure gathered and cataloged from her avid reading and rich experiences. A good wife's opinion is premium material.

A one-sided marriage, where the wife has complete recall or the husband thunders his masterful mandates, is in for stormy weather. Some of the happiest marriages are those in which stimulating conversations are enjoyed. Yet there is even a companionship of silence, in which it is enough just to be together, where the other's very presence is not only sufficient but sublime.

Pure companionship is not always enjoyed in the earlier years of the marriage because of the demands of the husband's profession and the wife's duties in their home. It is even more difficult to experience when both are working outside the home, attacking the problem of equalizing the supply and the demand. One day the value and importance of companionship will suddenly dawn upon you. Then you will know the joy of just having each other and being together, and you will discover that companionship is one of the greatest aspects of marriage.

Marriage is commitment. Each one should be wholly committed to the other. It can be categorically stated that marriage will not work without absolute commitment, not merely to the vows, the dreams, or an ideal, but also to each other. That is why both the bride and the groom say, "I take *thee* to be my wedded" one. As the months add up to years, each should be constantly moving to a deeper commitment.

12

Ever on Your Mind

I know your mind and heart are filled with thoughts of love for her. That is the way it should be, and that is the way it can always be. Furthermore, that is the way it is in a wonderful marriage. Possibly without being aware of it, you have changed your thinking pattern. What was once *I* and *mine* is now *we* and *ours*. This change is both significant and imperative. It must always be so.

Thoughtfulness is a simple word that includes a number of things. You need not be a millionaire or a magician to practice it. Naturally you will never be able to do all you want to do for your wife, for the budget will not permit that. The desires of your heart for her will far exceed your money. But thoughtfulness is best expressed in words and actions. An embrace, a loving look, a few beautifully chosen words are usually more cherished than a costly gift. Material items are not always the best evidence of love. In the midst of an exciting conversation at a birthday dinner

61

party, one woman looked lovingly at her husband and said, "Hi, honey, how are you, way over there?" The depth and vitality of her love were revealed in those few words and by the look in her eyes. This was loving thoughtfulness.

No man will forget the special days if he lives beyond himself and really loves his wife. He will remember these memorable occasions even in the midst of mountains of obligations and pressures. Every good husband knows that special days merit special treatment, and he will be delighted to have a reason to break the budget for the gift he has been wanting to give. No matter how long you have been married, an intimate gift, flowers, or a dinner out will delight her. Why wait for a special occasion? Little remembrances add romance to the marriage. Actually, little things at unexpected times are of great importance, because they tell her in a beautiful way that she is the queen in your heart.

Some husbands are so inconsiderate and romantically dull that an unexpected gift might be more than the wife could take. The shock could be too great! But all that our wives do for us and all that they mean to us warrant our extra expressions of thoughtfulness.

An integral part of true thoughtfulness is sensitivity—an awareness of how she feels and what she needs. It will not take you long to learn to read her heart; the thoughtful husband will respond accordingly. On certain days a comforting embrace and a load-lifting word are the remedy.

When you and your wife are present at an occasion, make certain that she is really a part of it. Thoughtfulness sees to it that the one you love is not only there but also is having a pleasant time. I will never forget how a friend, in the middle of a tense Scrabble game, got up and went over to his wife and simply said, "Hi, lover." She lit up like a Christmas tree. A thoughtful husband makes sure that his wife is involved, enjoying herself, and most of all that she knows he is delighted that she is there with him.

If thoughtfulness doesn't come naturally, cultivate the art. It is something of which a wife will never tire, for a woman never complains about her husband's attentiveness! It is another of the little things that can enhance your relationship. Use numerous ways to show and tell her that she is in your thoughts and heart.

The desire to please the one you love is one of the small keys that unlock the doors to a radiant marriage. If you always wish to please your wife above anyone else, including yourself, you are on your way to unfathomable happiness. It is not hard when you truly and deeply love each other.

If you are willing to listen to your beloved and see her point of view, you will have a bond that nothing can sever and that will add a dimension of delight to your marriage. Listening with undivided attention is a grace that too few cultivate. Far too often a husband is preoccupied with the burden of his responsibilities. Yet nothing is more important than talking things through until your wife is satisfied you understand and care.

Let me add a few more suggestions. You might call them "you don't have to's." You don't have to be right every time! Even if you are, you don't have to remind her of it. Heaven help the wife with a husband who has to win every discussion or be right on every issue or fact. I have met too many men who had to be right every time: I've tried to pick up the shattered pieces of their marriages. No man is that perfect. I can think of a number of men who should have listened to their wives. Pilate, for one! I will never be able to forget the time when my wife said to me, "I think you've taken the wrong road." The road that I, with manly pride, insisted was right, turned out to be a dead-end street. Being wrong and having to admit it may be an assault on a man's pride, but most of the male species are overweight with pride, anyway. A girl will supremely love a guy who can readily say either "I'm wrong" or "You're right."

Today we are caught up in the image syndrome. However, you need not impress anyone. One thing is certain: you don't have to impress your wife. She loves you for what you are, for what she sees in you, and for what comes forth from the treasury of your personality. Some need to alter the impression that they try to make. Most people can easily spot the impression act and are turned off completely, for it is the mark of a real phony. Seeking to impress is basically a problem of the self-life that reveals a sense of personal inadequacy—a need that Christ is abundantly able to meet. Remember, every man has qualities that are attractive and appealing. It is important for you always to be yourself. Every man's calling requires it, and a wife rightfully demands it.

Another three-little-word sentence that will give you much love and appreciation is the sublime statement, "I am sorry." A man stands tall when he has learned to say it willingly and quickly, but some men would rather choke to death. In fact, men particularly find it difficult to say.

Some husbands think that to say these words is to eat "humble pie" and that humble pie is totally distasteful. Actually, humble pie is really a tasty morsel that nourishes an area of the personality usually on starvation rations or withering from malnutrition. I have had to eat my share, and I needed every bite. Plain stubbornness prevents scores of men from giving expression to these important words. Who dares to forget the verse from God, "Stubbornness is as iniquity and idolatry" (1 Samuel 15:23). After the first time, "I am sorry" is easier to say. Nor should it be a once-in-a-lifetime phrase, squeezed out under duress. Some men seem to feel that, having said it once, they have covered every time and situation. But this phrase, like forgiveness, is a seventy-times-seven proposition. The more willing we are to say it, the less we have to do so. Invariably, when we do, we are rewarded by loving responses from our wives.

Doubtless you have already conquered many things

that can be stumbling blocks to marital happiness. It is amazing how little things can hinder, but it is equally amazing how the use of these little suggestions can help.

13

Silence Is Not Always Golden

Silence is not always golden. Granted, we all talk too much! When you consider how we are made, with two eyes and two ears and one mouth, it should be clear that we should look and listen twice as much as we talk. The prevailing malady of many is foot-in-mouth disease. Many of our troubles are engineered by our words.

However, I'm convinced that in marriage, more difficulties stem from silence than from too many words. A pastor friend, who does considerable counseling, said the main reason for marital troubles is that "the lines of communication break down."

Some years ago I read an article entitled "When Silence Is Treason." The author suggested that a high official was guilty because he was tragically silent when an international treaty—one contrary to the Constitution and disastrous in the light of world unity and peace—had been secretly signed. There is a time in marriage when silence is criminal. Too often the wife's sad lament is "I get the silent treatment. He just clams up, and I go through the hours in agonizing wonder, my heart filled with a score of fears!" Nothing is right about that. Communicate! That's a basic rule, because you cannot have a successful marriage without it.

Communication means sharing. Naturally it means talking about the day's activities, accomplishments, and demands, as well as the shots you dubbed at work. Your partner needs and has a right to know your thoughts and feelings. Silence is an aggravation that compounds fears. A woman needs the excitement of a challenge, so bare your heart to her. Most women have the spirit and the stamina to attempt any challenge with you. In such an hour of sharing you will find what a truly remarkable woman you have been given.

As time moves on, you will find that your wife is an invaluable sounding board for concepts you want to present to your superiors. Recently a brilliant and successful administrator told me: "What a jewel I have in my wife! I've learned that if I can't sell her, my bosses will never buy the idea. I've come to greatly trust her opinions and impressions." This is a clue to the success of his marriage. He has made her a partner and counselor. She feels needed and a part of the decision making, and she is flattered that he will seek her wisdom.

In some homes the only conversation is the wife's whining complaint and the husband's uninterested grunts. The only talking in the average home today must be done during the television commercial. You can imagine how long and substantive that is! And then some couples wonder why their marriages are deteriorating!

Some couples communicate verbally only in time of conflict. Then the irritations stored through months come rushing out. In these times of tension, with the husband and wife standing eyeball to eyeball and tempers blazing, the thoughts expressed and the words used are inevitably destructive and de-humanizing. Not enough marriage partners have the maturity to discuss their differences openly and honestly. If there has not been time for talk before, it's too late to attempt anything productive during a crisis. Possibly the crisis could have been avoided if real time had been given to sharing each day's feelings of achievement, failure, or frustration.

Differences need discussion. If you are old enough to be married, you should be mature enough to talk through any matter. When there are differences, it is unwise to turn away or turn silent. You may not want to face up to what she has to say, but she will never forgive you if you refuse to hear her out. Take the time needed, and also use the oil of patience. Bring to the discussion a cool head and a warm heart!

Communication is not always conversation. It is more than words; it is a gesture or a glance. There are, as one keen analyst suggests, "the wavelengths of love." A woman can convey either sweet or scorching truths with her eyes. On the other side of the ledger, the look on your face can either crush her or bring her ecstasy. One tiny glance can speak clearly of love and protection and give her heart the serene sense of security.

Communication is more than listening; it is understanding and reacting. Every partner yearns for the other to understand his or her feelings and emotions. She wants something more than your attention. There must be responsiveness, true empathy, a sensitivity to her deep emotions. It should be a responsiveness brought about because you "feel" with her, so you reach out with words, feelings, and hands. It should be done quickly, with deep feeling and sincerity. It will tell her you care, and by that assurance she will be soothed by your words and comforted by your caress.

However, listening is a large part of communication. There are times to talk, but there is also a time to listen. The unique genius of one exciting conversationalist was her attentive listening. Nothing is more disconcerting or discourteous than to have a listener preoccupied with something or someone else when you are trying to talk to him. Therefore, honor your wife with your undivided attention as you listen. She merits it because she is the most important person in your life.

Begin your marriage with sharing everything. Those who really love always do. Life is filled with events of excitement that only can be enjoyed with someone else. As you talk together about both trivial things and consequential matters, trust and dependence will strengthen your marriage. The years together will bring experiences in which you will need each other's wisdom and the comfort of reassuring words. The times that you will treasure most will be those when you have bared your hearts to each other and where hands and eyes have communicated the beauty of your love.

14

Thanksgiving Every Day

A wife and mother, looking back over a highly successful marriage, put her finger on the secret when she said: "Even if I burned the biscuits, he never complained. I don't suppose he would have fussed at me if I'd burned the house down." This is a testimonial from a woman who had known fifty golden years of marital happiness. She and her husband had been sweethearts through it all—all the hard times, heartaches, and a crippling accident. Always there was a word of praise for her; no caustic criticism, no complaints, but always the encouraging and kindly word.

You should have seen the radiant look on a wife's face as she exclaimed, "He brought such joy to my heart!" It was a word of gratitude for the man in her life. Nothing sweetens a marriage like a word of thanks and a bit of sincere praise.

There are scores of reasons and seasons to bestow them. I would like to suggest it is best received when the day has gone awry, as when her prize cake falls or the roast burns. Even if you have to search for it, find something to say that will change the complexion of things. Don't let a day pass without a word of appreciation: that is a great rule. Even if she looks like an accident about to happen or as though her hair had been combed with an eggbeater, that's when she needs to hear she is beautiful in your eyes and you love her.

One of life's graces is the art of expressing appreciation, and the best place to cultivate it is in the home. Who needs or deserves it more than your wife? You can tell her how great the meal was, how beautifully she keeps the home, and of course how lovely she is. This has the double effect of challenging her to do and be all of these things and also encouraging her in what she has done.

I have never seen anyone who wasn't stimulated by praise. I've listened to volumes of complaints about a foreman's lack of appreciation for the laborer's hard work. You learn to expect that; but the amazing thing is the huge deficit of praise in the home. It is strange that a junior or senior executive will quickly praise someone who works a forty-hour week for him, yet be wholly neglectful of his wife, who shares his burdens of life.

You need not wait for an occasion. Praise is something you can give generously in season and out of season. At unexpected times, and even on occasions when undeserved, you can offer words of gratefulness. Of course, when there has been a special achievement, you should not miss the opportunity for a compliment, publicly or privately.

Have you ever noticed what an athlete will endure for an Olympic gold medal? Translate that into the living out of a marriage. There is nothing your wife won't attempt, no matter how tedious or trying, if there is a laurel of praise at the end of the struggle.

Praise and gratitude are truly sweet and appreciated, so be generous with them. If you want the sugar of affection, give her a reason for giving it. Too many men want to be on the receiving end, but rarely show gratitude for all their wives have done.

It is also true that the oil of praise can smooth a lot of marital trouble. In fact, if gratitude had been expressed to begin with, the tempest might have been avoided. You can accomplish more with praise than with complaint.

There is rarely any need for criticism. Some things will never change, so it is useless to work up a head of steam over them. What changes can be made are best accomplished by magnifying your wife's excellent qualities. When a girl is showered with praise, she will do everything in her power to please you. Who can ask for more?

Thankfulness and praise will get you somewhere —right in the center of her heart!

15

"Patience, Brother!"

Patience is a word that has a bigger place in marriage than many realize. But patience is a quality given little or no consideration, especially in the thoughts of young couples contemplating marriage. It may seem trivial, but it is of paramount importance. Marriage may be your cup of tea, but patience is the sugar needed for its enjoyment. Remember that bit of musical wisdom, "A spoonful of sugar makes the medicine go down." Marriage is not medicine, but there are some things in it that you may find hard to swallow. The sugar of patience goes a long way to sweeten the taste.

Daily portions of patience are needed for a number of reasons. First, things are not always going to work out as you expect, no matter how carefully you plan them. The best laid plans of mice and men go awry, and when they do, let patience be the soothing zephyr to cool the temper. I have noticed over the years that it is when the little plans and designs fail that men become most impatient. Temper seems to rise over trivial failures or disruptions, although matters of consequence can be handled with grace.

There is another conundrum. We become most impatient with those we profess to love. I have seen men take out their irritations or frustrations on their families and act as if their loved ones are supposed to grin and bear it. My deep conviction is that if your wife is the queen of your heart, she should always be treated as one—not just when it suits you or your disposition. The important virtue of patience is often strangely lacking when it should be abundantly operative in a Christian's life. Let your life be challenged by Paul's prayer in Colossians 1:10-11: "That ye might walk worthy of the Lord . . . strengthened with all might . . . unto all patience." The strengthening of the Lord is to result in patience.

There is another reason for patience. Your wife may be the sweetest in the world, but sometimes and in several ways she is bound to irritate you. Again, a woman is different! When God created her, He used a rib from a man, but the similarity stops there. A woman's makeup, emotions, thought patterns, and reasoning are vastly different from a man's. You are going to need patience again and again, not because your chosen one is something less than perfect, but simply because she's a woman and you are a man.

Before you mistake this idea for a concept of superiority and rush to accept it as an accolade of praise, remember that most men are needy souls, possessing their share of quirks and flaws. If wives were to bare their hearts, doubtless we would see how much patience they constantly exercise. Honestly, I see more of it in women! I saw a marriage change from a pending, horrible disaster to a thing of joy and beauty simply through the great and skillful patience of a young wife.

For several weeks I watched a man who was the epitome of impatience. His marked impatience was directed at almost everyone and anyone, but particularly at his family. I learned two lasting lessons from him. First, temper and impatience go hand in hand. He had a "short fuse" and could erupt quickly and violently. There is no way a Christian can justify or excuse temper, for the Word of God classifies it as sin and includes it in the catalog of the works of the flesh. If patience is to have her perfect work, temper has to be held in check by means of the indwelling Spirit.

The second lesson was even more pronounced. His impatience was directed at the things that affected *his* plans, desires, or schedule. Like a neon sign, it spelled out *self* in bold letters. It clearly outlined that everything had to revolve around him and please him. This attitude hangs a yoke that is too heavy to bear around a wife's neck. Obviously this egocentric kind of life has no place in a believer's life.

From the biblical point of view, patience has surprising prominence. James, a man with a pastor's heart, wrote the phrase I mentioned earlier: "Let patience have her perfect work" (James 1:4). You cannot miss what that says. A little patience is not enough! You will need all you can get for every day and every situation. Peter (and who should know better the need and importance of patience?) wrote: add patience to self-control and godliness to patience (see 2 Peter 1:6, ASV). Patience is one link in the golden chain of faith. With good reason, Peter puts it between self-control and godliness, suggesting that if you do not have patience, you have failed in both self-control and godliness.

Because of his impatience, King Saul preempted the privileges that belonged to the priesthood; his act cost him his kingdom. That is a high price to pay for impatience! I have been an eyewitness to the dethroning of a husband in a woman's heart, and a large part of her decision was due to his impatience. His continuous outbursts of impatience ate away at the marriage. Coupled with sudden and repeated bursts of temper, it was understandable why the marriage was badly mangled.

My advice to any prospective groom is, "Ye have need of patience" (Hebrews 10:36). Everyone does. If you cannot exercise it, your marriage is potentially in trouble. More than that, you need God's grace to work in your heart. Basically, the amount of patience possessed and expressed is the test of a person's spiritual health. Most significantly, it reveals his spiritual condition and true relationship with Christ.

On the other hand, I have seen great benefits from the practice of patience. Invariably it brings joy to the heart, peace to the home, and a sense of harmony to the marriage. I will never forget the wisdom of a man whose marriage was pure delight. "For every ounce of patience expressed to my wife, I've reaped a ton of affection, kindness, and thoughtfulness," he said. "There were times when the easiest thing would have been to blurt out my irritation, let my temper go. I reasoned if Job could be patient with all he endured, then nothing I would ever experience should prompt me to impatience. If an Old Testament saint could be characterized by patience, then, as a true believer, it should be a marked characteristic of my life."

Patience in the home and with those you love proves the genuineness and depth of your faith and provides some of marriage's greatest rewards.

16

"There'll Be Some Changes Made"

Remember the song entitled "There'll be some changes made"? To make changes is apparently the purpose of some marriages. Maybe I am prejudiced, but it seems that the female has a greater tendency to engineer changes. Possibly when she fell in love she saw a diamond in the rough, a chunk of beautiful marble with great potential. For her there was a challenge—possibly more challenge than love! Perhaps the girl was not really deeply in love with the man, but instead, in love with what she thought she could make out of him. In many instances the work was done by the chisel of hard words and the abrasive of a rough tongue.

Doubtless, changes are needed in the partners of any marriage. At this moment of your courtship, you probably would challenge this statement, for no doubt you are convinced that she is the perfect girl. You are positive that there is not a flaw or imperfection in this jewel that you have found. I hope you will always feel this way. In the eyes of love, that which might otherwise loom as an insurmountable fault is easily overlooked. Love covers a multitude of wrongs or flaws.

However, I have never seen a marriage where there were not a few adjustments to be made—a little give and take on the part of each one. Most adjustments are made with ease and grace. A man has to be either a supreme egotist or terribly myopic to be unaware that some changes need to be made in him. Sometimes parents fail to mold and fashion the child when he is in his formative years. Weak and doting parents often refused to see anything but perfection in a son or daughter. In such cases, it takes a lot of delicate skill by one partner to make any change in the other. Some changes are needed because, in spite of all the energy expended by loving parents, the child displayed stubborn resistance. I have seen amazing transformation in a man, changing him from a granitelike, grotesque character to an attractive personality. It was accomplished by the deft strokes of a loving wife using tools of tender, loving care.

Some men balk like a maverick at the thought of change. They are determined not to be harnessed. This stubbornness is usually the result of what they have witnessed as children; they have seen someone they loved beaten, badgered, broken, and saddled. This should never happen. One great asset of life is the willingness to take loving suggestions. I have frequently wondered why some are willing to take suggestions from their friends but reject all suggestions made by those who really loved them.

Upon serious reflection, most husbands would readily admit that the changes made in their lives were for their betterment. They were accomplished in loving ways, with grace and kindness. It was done so deftly that the husband scarcely realized when his wife had chipped off a rough spot. Yet after her artisanry had taken place, that part of his character never again seemed to jab those with whom he worked.

You will discover that some things will not change. One of the greatest bits of wisdom I ever discovered was simply "What you cannot change, accept with grace." Do not allow it to become a mountain when it is only a mound. If you will keep your love for your loved one glowing, no flaw or fault will dim the luster of her loveliness. Yet suppose it is a monumental fault, like leaving the cap off the toothpaste or being habitually tardy. Satirical? Obviously these things are trivial. But such ridiculous things have thrown roadblocks into some marriages. Believe me, all the great qualities—all the love, the charm, the tender care, the undergirding of her strength of personality —far outweigh those things that resist change.

It is highly probable that part of the God-given role of the wife, as helpmeet, is to effect some needed changes in a husband. Not that the wife has a special skill for producing change; rather, because of her tremendous love, she has the tender touch to which her husband will submit. It always helps to remember that whatever she does, it is because you are everything to her, almost her very life! Naturally she wants the one she loves to be greatly admired by all. A simple truth will guarantee success in the process of change: be willing to change because of your desire to be all that your loving partner wants you to be.

17

Keep the Two R's in Marriage

How much serious thought have you given to your upcoming marriage? Most people in love do not think very seriously about the details of marriage. They only know they want to be married, and they are confident their life together will be all they could desire it to be. This dream-world attitude rejects the possibility of problems and dismisses the thought that serious consideration of those problems is needed prior to the "I do's." Prior to assenting to perform the wedding ceremony, I have asked many young people to define the ingredients of a happy and successful marriage. Too often the only response was a shrug and a smile or an "I guess" answer, devoid of any prior thought. High on the list of answers I have received was this simple yet sublime statement: "a lot of love."

I am not challenging the supreme importance of love. But here I want to consider the necessity of keeping romance and responsibility in marriage, to reinforce and beautify it.

First, *romance*. Romance includes imagination, excitement, and adventuresomeness. The unexpected and beyond-the-call-of-duty thoughtful words and deeds are important. Endearing phrases make a marriage wonderful; no wife ever tires of hearing them. Deeds add harmony to the refrain, making beautiful music! The little deed at the unexpected time leaves a lovely and lasting imprint on her heart.

One of the nevers of a successful marriage is to forget your anniversary. Of course you will remember her birthday, even when she arrives at the age when she is thirty-nine and holding.

These romantic things, little though they may be, boldly declare your deep devotion and lasting love. A lovely and gracious woman, remembering the singular beauty of her marriage, said, "It was thirty-six years of a perfect marriage." The years were made perfect by the unexpected little things her husband did, like bringing home flowers when it wasn't her birthday.

I stayed in a home where funds were meager, but the wife, her eyes made radiant by love, showed me a card her husband had left on her dresser. It was a tiny thing that made a big impression. Another couple, who had kept the fire of love glowing, used one night a week, if at all possible, just to be together. They made these occasions special times as they enjoyed an excellent restaurant or some choice entertainment. Any girl enjoys a date with her loved one, after the wedding as well as before. Marriage is meant to be not only a great arrangement but also an exciting adventure.

At the other end of the spectrum is *responsibility*. When you say the vows, you enter a new phase of your life. With only a few words you have suddenly become a husband and provider. It is your responsibility to have money in the bank and bread on the table, for your wife is looking to you for sustenance and security. That security comes from more than an arm about her shoulder or even your shoulder to cry on; it comes from knowing she can count on you for every material and physical need. A wife needs security, and she will find it if she has the assurance, because of your dependability, that you will do your best to meet every need.

Review the records, and you will find that numerous marriages failed because the husband refused to assume the role of provider. Generally it is a matter of immaturity; he wants the benefits without the responsibility. There is more to a marriage than giving of yourself or sharing your love. Though vital, they are inadequate if you fail to provide the daily bread, other necessities, plus a few luxuries. Your work must take priority so the needs of the home will be met, for it is here that the wife finds so much of her security.

A true husband knows that his responsibilities extend beyond that of being the breadwinner. He is responsible for his wife's happiness, security, and contentment. You are called upon to be the kind of a man in whom she can always believe, the kind of husband of whom she can always be immensely proud, and one worthy of her adoration.

Long before you reach the altar you should have contemplated this new role in your life. In the days of courtship you have been moving toward this new plateau of maturity. Most young men thrive under the challenge and opportunity of being a husband. It takes a lot of earthly effort, along with the blessings of heaven, to make your marriage all you want it to be.

Many marriages have substituted *routine* for *romance.* The glorious adventure and the ecstasy and excitement are gone. In some instances it did not take long to happen.

There has to be an explanation. It goes without saying that either the basics were missing or something damaged the foundation. The right kind of marriage does not disintegrate to an arrangement where one is the breadwinner and the other the housekeeper. I talked with a disillusioned young mother, surrounded by the clutter in her home and two sets of diapers on the line. She lamented, "I knew what love was, but I surely didn't know what marriage was all about." It had taken only three years to dismantle the beauty of her marriage. She felt neglected—more like a servant than a sweetheart—and doubtless she was. Inwardly she felt trapped. She could only see dishes, diapers, dirt, and the duties of being a wife. She was about ready to put *revolt* into her marriage. It wasn't all one-sided. Not only had her husband neglected her; she had neglected herself.

The condition of near revolt doesn't just suddenly happen. It begins with little acts of carelessness, and the next step is the attitude of taking the other one for granted. It is amazing how quickly one can slip into this sad condition.

A man, in honor of his city's centennial celebration, wore a bushy beard. Someone teased him, saying that if he didn't shave, he would never get a kiss. His honest reply was "It's been such a long time since I've been kissed, I wouldn't know what one tasted like anyway." In his case, romance had been replaced by rust. The marriage was screeching as the wheels turned. They not only didn't need each other; they did not really care. Completely dismissing the Lord's purpose in marriage, they missed the joy that sweetens marriage with every new experience and the passing of the years.

Two other things not needed in marriage are the rough and the rocky. Nothing is charming about a rocky road in marriage, and far too many couples travel this route. Usually all the guidelines were ignored as the partners struck out across the uncharted prairie of their marriage. All was springtime when they began, but suddenly summertime was long and hot, some of the flowers of love began to wilt, and the way roughened. What began as a minor drifting apart became a major breach, which opened the way for a large incident, an indiscretion or involvement, to sever the marriage bond.

I have a vivid memory of one couple who came to

88

see me. The wife said, "All the love I had for him is gone. He killed it." What a rocky road was described as she recounted the details of her marital catastrophe! It took a miracle to rekindle the love, but the Lord found an ember left that He could use. They labored hard to put the pieces back together. I learned two great lessons as I watched them. First, the marriage is rarely the same, not as smooth or sweet as before the disruption. Second, by God's grace, there is a way back, but the road is long and difficult. This was recently emphasized as I listened to a man share his marital disappointment. He was having an acute inner struggle to forgive and forget, because the memory of the incident that drove him from home was too vivid. It is well to remember that only God can both forgive and forget. Every man has to live with his memory, and that is agonizing. Here is an axiom: never allow a word to be said or an act committed that requires either partner to expend great portions of forgiveness.

Giant trees have been toppled by buffeting winds when there was no taproot. If the marriage only has the surface roots of love, attraction, and complementing qualities, it will not stand life's storms. However, these surface roots are needed as feeder roots, and every marriage must have them to give it vitality and beauty. Yet it is the taproot that gives stability. Obviously, in marriage, the taproot is the spiritual element. No one can eliminate the spiritual without compounding his troubles. A marriage is more than physical or emotional; it must have the spiritual element as the source of strength and cohesiveness.

Christ, central in the marriage as in every phase of life, is a basic necessity. That is the essence of His declaration that He is the bread of life and can give us living water. There is no life apart from Him. Christ is not a luxury, someone nice to know, an added pleasure. He is an absolute essential for all of life, particularly for the vitality of a marriage.

A marriage in which the spiritual element is strong cannot be destroyed and will not disintegrate. The spiritual is a preventive. A major breach will not take place when the Saviour is supreme in the home, for Christ has a way of cementing hearts together so that neither time, tests, nor temptations can sever them.

A true wife is like a treasure: the longer you live with her, the more you will discover about her priceless value. New beauty will be brought to light by each experience. There will be a loveliness, a grace, a strength of character that unfold from within her as you experience sorrow or difficulty. The longer you walk together and the deeper the valleys in your journey, the more of the beautiful mystery of womanhood will be revealed to you. There is nothing routine about a real woman. You will never fully fathom women, but then, who wants to? It is their mystery that adds tang to the marriage.

18

Sacred Trust

One of these glad days the courtship will be over. Your response to that fact is "Hasten the day!" At one time there was some competition for her affection, but that decreased after you looked into each other's eyes and said those all-important words, "I love you!" Competition is not a factor since you put that diamond on her hand. However, from the moment you say "I do," all rivalry for affection ceases forever. How could it be any other way?

There is a five-letter word that is basic to any marriage—*trust*. I learned the profound importance of this word from the rough and tough colonel under whom I served in World War II. I had brought a young, deeply disturbed, impetuous soldier to see him. Nothing I had said to the young man would satisfy him or bring him back to reality. A "dear John" letter had blown his hopes and dreams, and he was demanding a stateside furlough so he could "beat some sense into her head." I am sure the emphasis was on *beat*. The

91

usually terse and gruff colonel listened carefully and then said gently, "Son, you don't have a marriage anymore." He went on to explain wisely that when trust is shattered, the marriage is destroyed. That is wisdom at its best.

There are several ways that trust can be either scarred or broken in pieces. Infidelity can ruin all the trust of the best, most loving marriage. It is also a fact that once the trust is taken from the marriage by unfaithfulness, it is almost impossible to restore it. I talked for hours to a close friend, who said out of the depths of a broken heart, "Our marriage will never be the same."

Marriage, like fine china, is delicate. It is easily chipped or broken when there is unfaithfulness. Granted, the "I'm sorry's" and true, repentant promises are wonderful cohesives. Yet it is difficult to put the marriage together again and make it stick. If the marriage is put under intense heat by new difficulties or deep differences, the epoxy won't hold.

Numerous marriages, even those breached by infidelity, are restored, and the partners find true and lasting happiness. The Lord's grace is wonderfully operative in the crucial times of marriage trauma. A couple really committed to Christ can work through such a crisis and make something wonderful out of the seemingly shattered pieces. Even so, a certain amount of the initial sweetness and solidity will be missing. It is not all that Christ meant it to be; that is part of the wage of the sin.

I am not minimizing Christ's restorative power. Also, I am not discounting the Great Physician's healing touch on the wounds of marriage, for our Lord can do anything. Yet you must reckon with memory. Standing on the quarterdeck of our troop transport, an officer lamented, "If only I could erase the memory of that one night. But it's always there." In the Lord's parable of Luke 16:19-31, there are these grave words: "Son, remember!" Memory can be tormenting and punitive. When God forgives, He forgets; but man has trouble forgetting. Often the vivid picture stays in the mind. Even God's forgiveness, real as it is, and the partner's forgiveness, sincere as it may be, cannot wipe out the memory of an unfaithful act.

Trust can be weakened by so-called flirtation—an act, a look, or a word. Keep your eyes where your heart is. It is no wonder that so many marriages are either dissolved or lived out in discord, for today both men and women are too free with words and too careless in their actions. There may be nothing dishonorable meant in any affectionate word or a friendly embrace, but it may weaken trust. In a true marriage, each should live and act in such a way that trust is never put in jeopardy.

The best advice I know is: guard trust as zealously as you would the Gospel, for it is sacred. This five-letter word is worth more than a fortune, because it pays constant dividends in boundless joy and love.

19

"Man Your Battle Stations!"

Man your battle stations! Any old navy salt knows that is the cry when a skirmish is about to begin. How many times is this the atmosphere of the home when tempers are flaring and the "fire in the eyes" gives warning! Far too many marriages are constant feuds. Others erupt only occasionally, but with a mighty volley. Some may argue that this is a normal situation, but I challenge the concept that a marriage has to have its battles. Naturally there will be differences. No two people, even with identical backgrounds, are always going to agree on everything. Yet the differences need not result in a free-for-all.

I think some couples allow themselves to wage occasional warfare just because they have been told so often by so many that battles are a normal part of married life. Usually they have been witnesses to the battles of their parents. Unfortunately, they do not know that marriage is meant to be different and can be! Some of the learned scholars of our day suggest that since opposites attract, they make the ideal marriage. But it is equally true that when opposites come together, the result can be an explosion. This situation, which explains the continual warfare in some marriages, makes the home a battleground. Of course some temperaments have not been tempered by the Spirit, and this lack makes for conflict.

There are sociologists and marriage counselors who emphasize the importance of husband and wife being alike in disposition and desires. It is true that in many homes that are wonderfully happy both the husband and wife like the same things.

There is also the utter nonsense of how wonderful it is to make up after a battle. The truth is, some of the verbal barbs expressed in the heat of the fight are the seed thoughts that trigger the next barrage. Often these conflicts increase in number and intensity. Although the couple may kiss and make up, frequently the hurt and bitterness linger. Wounds suffered in the exchange do not lie dormant but grow malignant.

I have seen many people literally weep about their marriages. Only a little perception was needed to look through their tears to the deep hurt in their hearts—hurt that had been there for years. The constant ache from these wounds had destroyed much of the loveliness in the marriage. More than a few "forgive me's" are required to heal the inner wounds resulting from battles between husband and wife.

All too often I have been called in to be the referee in a family fight. As I look back, it is apparent that most battles were due to the couple's ignorance of Christian meekness. One would think that something so evident in the life of the Lord Jesus and included in the cluster of the fruit of the Spirit would be both known and possessed. After looking for a long time for a good definition of meekness, I decided the best is "the relinquishing of your rights." In family battles it is usually a matter of rights, given expression in such terms as "wanting his or her way." Christ is the solution here, as in every problem of the heart and soul. As we yield fully to the Lord and as the Holy Spirit operates in our lives, meekness can be the master of the situation. There can be no doubt that most fights could be avoided if, in love, we relinquished our rights. No one really knows how many blessings could be brought into the home if this choice segment of the fruit of the Spirit was utilized.

Prayer changes things—both situations and people. Suppose some ugly thing does well up in the heart? What if the heart feels it will burst if this thing is not expressed? Why not tell it to God, aloud and on your knees, with your partner listening? Just try telling God how despicable she or he is. Right. You can't! On your knees you get a new perspective. Being on your knees also shuts off temper in a strange and marvelous way. Even more, on your knees you will feel the full impact of your own words, and then you will find it impossible to lash out verbally.

When God has brought together two loving hearts, so fully yielded to the power of the Holy Spirit that fruit can be produced, then yours can be a home that knows constant harmony and wonderful happiness. The old cliché is true: it takes two to fight. And may I also add, it takes two to love. It seems there is a choice either to fight or to love. Why not love? It's a lot more fun!

20

Dollars and Sense

Currently you have marriage on your mind, and that is about all. When you suddenly come down out of the clouds you will find there are groceries to buy and payments to make. It will be a new experience. You may find that there are so many necessities that it is a struggle to make ends meet. You will be experiencing the truth that "two can live as cheaply as one, but for only half as long!"

One of the greatest aggravations in marriage is finances. Most counselors agree that money problems can stifle love and understanding, rapidly causing more sudden and serious domestic discord than anything else.

The solution is not necessarily in having abundance; yet it surely helps to always have enough. Of course the promise of Scripture is "God shall supply all your need according to his riches in glory" (Philippians 4:19), and the Lord's provision is something on which a Christian can truly count. Your job opportunities may mean a restricted and limited income, but you are not alone. That is where most people live, so you have joined the throng of those who are in pursuit of making ends meet. A strange paradox about finances is that there seems to be such a long time between paychecks and such a short time between payment demands.

Financial solvency is possible if you can adopt a fiscal policy that both you and your wife agree on, and then honor it faithfully. It is wrong for a wife to live in financial ignorance of the family income. Some men try to justify their secretiveness by saying they want to shield the wife from worry. Often this protectiveness is the veneer that hides an ulterior motive. Finances are not the husband's exclusive province. Usually one partner is a better money manager. If it is the wife, yield this area of the marriage to her, and do it gladly. Then you will have more time to achieve other goals and be free to take care of the demanding aspects of your occupation.

The total financial picture should be known by both partners; there must be no secret or hidden accounts. If togetherness is important in other areas of marriage, it is imperative here. In some marriages when both husband and wife are working, a "yours and mine" complex develops. This attitude of independence can cause a crack in the foundation of marital success. A happy marriage demands interdependence, a needing of each other. *Yours* and *mine* are words that do not belong in the vocabulary of marriage. When the

99

vows are said, from then on it is ours. All available dollars are to be owned equally.

You can count on one thing, namely, the unexpected expense. A financial beatitude says, "Blessed is the man who expects the unexpected, for he will not be disappointed." There is a proverbial rainy day for every couple, and some seem to live in a perpetual storm. For this reason, it is wise to plan for it. That means you don't spend all you make all the time. With credit buying and with all the needs a newly married couple have, it is easy to become hopelessly in debt. The average family has more payments than they can make. Here is one area where you dare not come up to average. As a Christian, nothing is more destructive to your witness than financial carelessness or fiscal irresponsibility.

Some find success in adopting a budget. Home finances need to be worked out, taking ample time for discussion. Even some of the best budgets have to bend, so don't be too rigid.

An old tune says, "I wish I was single again, for when I was single, my pockets did jingle. I wish I was single again." Remember, it can be true for both partners. Your wife needs to have some money jingling in her purse. I know of a couple who found the road to romance mighty rough, owing to the husband's demand for an exact accounting of every penny. He demanded far more of his wife than he demanded of himself. There was barely enough for her needs, but always enough for his desires. When you boil that down, nothing but selfishness is left. That is too bitter for any wife to swallow.

A second couple's difficulty was acute stinginess. The wife had to beg for the necessities of the home, food for the table, and clothes for the children; yet there was plenty in the bank. Nothing is more demoralizing for a wife than to have to plead for enough money to keep the home functioning. One wife's agonizing account revealed that she had to sneak a few dollars for herself. She exclaimed, "I'm tired of feeling like a thief and being treated like a servant."

Usually the wife is better at managing the money in the market and cutting the cost at the meat counter than the husband will ever be. Beyond the basic needs of living, the wife should have a certain amount to do with as she pleases. She will usually spend it on something that is ultimately designed to make her more attractive to you. Believe me, whatever it costs, it is worth it! It is all wrong for a husband to overlook the needs of his wife. Without controversy, our women are worth more than we can ever give them.

21

In-Laws: Problem or Asset?

If you could talk to 70 percent of all married couples, you would hear the complaint, "They ought to outlaw the in-laws." It is amazing that such a high percentage of marriages have acute and constant in-law problems. It can be partially explained, but not justified. It is hard for some parents to give a child to someone else. There is a terrible possessiveness that plagues others. I knew of one mother-in-law who was a considerable burr at times because she was reluctant to have her daughter lose her original family identity through marriage.

As you know, there is a volume of witticisms about the mother-in-law. Nine out of ten complaints about the mother-in-law come from the daughter-in-law. That being true, it is only natural that she should become the butt of the jokes. In doing some research, I found amazing agreement that the real culprit is indeed the husband's mother. The core of the problem is that two women have affection and attachment for one man. That constitutes no small problem!

Just having in-laws may be bad enough, but it is money in the bank compared to the potential difficulties if you have to live with them for a while. Be it ever so humble, there's no place like home, particularly when it's your own. It is equally true that, be it ever so large, no home is big enough for two families, regardless of how much you love one another. Problems mount when you share the stove and sink, but the really volatile situation exists when there are children to be trained.

On the whole, grandparents are notoriously inept at rearing grandchildren. It is questionable whether they did such a phenomenal job on their own children, yet somehow they feel supremely qualified when it comes to their second generation offspring. Usually they are terribly permissive. After all, as one grandfather said, "The only reason God made grandfathers was to spoil grandchildren!"

But like it or not, in-laws are inevitable. You are marrying into her family, and she, into yours. Hopefully, both sets of parents are gaining. One thing is not inevitable: in-laws do not have to be a problem. In fact, 25 percent of marriages are free of difficulties in this area.

The average mother-in-law is characterized as a middle-aged women who is maladjusted, lonely, and frustrated; she craves attention and needs affection. This description ought to say something to her husband! He **is the key** to taming this mother-in-law instinct.

Maybe if you understand the problem it will be easier to live with it. Absence not only makes the heart grow fonder; it also lessens the in-law problem. Distance can make a big difference, and I must confess I have recommended it more than a few times.

There are two things to remember. One, your in-laws have loved the one you now love for much longer than you have. That fact will never change, and it never should. Second, give the in-laws opportunities to continue this love relationship. There are ways for you to make it easy for them to include you in their love. Nothing does it so successfully or quickly as expressing your appreciation for their daughter. After all, they produced the girl you love, and what a tremendous achievement that was! Tell them what a great job they did. If you are always good to their daughter, they will love you for it. This fact was particularly shown to me by the way my grandfather loved my dad, for no son-in-law was ever better to a wife.

Any son-in-law—even one with merely marginal intelligence—should be smart enough to extend courtesy and kindness. It never hurts to show your love for your wife's parents. It can be all downhill for you in this area, for most in-laws are really anxious to be loved by you and to love you.

22

You Two, and Christ

I have often wondered how many engaged couples take time to seriously consider the spiritual aspects of marriage. Maybe they neglect this because they are caught up with love and living in a love-filled world. Unfortunately, their actions are probably evidence of the actual spiritual condition of their lives. Since Christ is incidental to them, He is ignored in the marriage plans. Christ must have a central place in your marriage. If the Lord brought you together, and I am sure He did, then He deserves the place of preeminence and the throne of sovereignty. Christ must be more than the unseen Host in the home; He is to be the recognized and reigning Master.

Much has been written about Christ as the foundation of marriage. This truth cannot be overemphasized. I have rarely seen a successful marriage that was not built solidly on Christ and where a vital relationship with Him was not maintained. Foundations, although essential, are made of simple ingredients. In marriage, these ingredients are a dynamic faith in Christ matched with equal proportions of prayer and the Word. Naturally Christ's mind will be sought and His will obeyed. Only Christ's presence and blessing can make the marriage perfect.

Obviously some marriages make it without Him; yet I am convinced it is a struggle much of the way. You might be surprised at what sometimes goes on behind the facade of a so-called perfect marriage. The story that the walls would tell, could they speak, would be one of constant tempest and conflict. I recall one such marriage in which the bold chidings of a teenage daughter, in mild revolt, smeared the picture her parents had painted before their friends. Their marriage was far from ideal. Their ardent admirers were shocked to learn that, within the privacy of the home, tempers flared and barbed, cutting words were flung, like javelins, to pin each other to the wall. The obvious explanation for the havoc was that Christ was not supreme in either their lives or in the marriage. They had, I suppose, sought His blessing at the beginning, but as the days added up to years, the Lord became secondary. They were trying to manage without the Master. One by-product was spiritual stagnation. Many apparently forget—if they ever knew—that one of the goals of a Christian marriage is spiritual maturity, whereby in the mutual strengthening of each other, the full stature of the Christ life is realized. This happens only when Christ has His rightful place.

A marriage needs Christ for every day, every activity, and every situation. He must be central in the marriage. It is when we look to Him daily in every situation that we shall know real blessing. A great many couples who would want to be classified as Christians only want Christ in a crisis. There is no question that the storms of life are too powerful for any couple to handle alone. Real wisdom should lead you to cultivate a fellowship with Christ so that you are confident of His help in every exigency.

In a world like ours, and with life as fragile as it is, how can anyone live without Christ supreme in his marriage? Not only in the dark and lonely hours do you need the refuge of the arms of Christ. Not only in calamity do you need the comfort of His presence. You need Christ daily and constantly. It is true that if you know Him—really know Him—you want Him with you all the way.

How great it is that He is always there in a crisis! If you check the divine record carefully, you will find that Christ was the answer in every crucial moment. Recall the Gospel narrative as it tells of a distraught father who found in Christ the comfort and help he desperately needed. And of course Christ touched his daughter. Needs of every kind were met by the Saviour in Cana as well as in Bethany. When needs and difficulties engulf you, there is quieting and comforting confidence in the power and help of the living Lord. Those yesterdays and our todays are the same to Him. Every experienced traveler along the way of life has found that marriage, with all its thrill and wonder, is made up of tests and struggles, problems and difficulties, so that every couple constantly needs Christ near. I cannot think of a day that can be lived without Him or one that is not made better by His presence.

Let me share two important truths I have discovered. First, when Christ in all His fullness and reality is in your life, the love you possess for your partner is deeper, richer, and fuller. Right now, in the glow of courtship love, you might challenge me, asserting that you couldn't love her more. Yet you can, and I think you will! Actually, it depends on how vital your relationship is with Christ. It is an absolute that the degree of our love for the one we profess to love is determined by the depth of our walk with Christ.

The second concept is that the more vital one's daily experience with Christ, the more one discovers of the victorious life, and the better partner he is in marriage. I can think of several such marriages, but let me tell of one. She was a superior mother and fantastic wife who walked close by Christ's side. This intimate fellowship with Christ and deep knowledge of Him made her the mother and wife that she was. You see, a close walk with Christ is not ethereal or insignificant. It will affect you in every area of your life, particularly in the love you have for the one the Lord has given you. You will be a better man, a more responsive mate, a more capable husband, and a more gracious lover if your relationship with Christ is deep and dynamic.

I heard a husband comment, as he evaluated the deep spiritual experience that his wife had had with Christ, "She's a better wife, mother, and helpmeet. She is better in every way and in every area of our marriage!" The impact of this statement was even greater because I knew that his wife was far above average even before her transforming encounter. There is a challenge here: go deep with Christ. Go very deep, not for what you will get from it, although the jewels of Christian life are found in the depths, but for what it will make you. Seek with all your heart a close walk with the Lord, an intimate relationship with our Saviour. That is where true happiness and blessing are found.

Beauty and loveliness are in marriage when Christ has His place. You can put it in a few words. When Christ is the foundation of the marriage, when He has a supreme and central place, you will have the best there is. This, too, is a "narrow way," and there are few who find it. Above all else, my son, find it. Do not settle for something less than God's best for your marriage.

23

Her Dad's Viewpoint

A marriage concept that I had never really thought about has just arrested my attention. The more I observed a demonstration and then reflected upon it, the louder it shouted, "Wait, think it over!"

Let me tell you what prompted it. I had spent part of a week with a wonderfully sincere and godly pastor whose two daughters had a very special place in his heart. (Most daughters do!) Actually, I guess it was what he did not say about their marriages that started the mental gears in motion. This man never came right out and said it—not a word of complaint. But in the privacy of his heart there was a secret grief because what he wanted for them and knew they deserved was missing in their marriages.

Suddenly I saw marriage from the point of view of the father-in-law, the way any dad feels who has given a young man the priceless treasure of his daughter. A worthy father, who has provided his daughter the best he can afford, will never be satisfied for her to have something less. I am not talking about material things only, but also about the intangibles that overflow from a loving heart.

As I reflected upon it, another experience exploded before me. A brilliant doctor, the father of three lovely daughters, expressed his concern: "If I could only be sure that these guys will give my daughters the love, care, and appreciation they need and deserve, then I could be content. But how do I know they will?" Again, I saw the marriage through the eyes of the girl's father.

Let me go back to the lesson I learned from my pastor friend. As I began to put the pieces together, the picture began to take shape. Some essential elements were missing in these marriages—a hint of neglect, a lack of consideration. One of the husbands was totally wrapped up in himself; life had to revolve around his interests and desires. The other husband was dominated by a demanding mother, who robbed the wife of her rightful place in her husband's heart. Even I noticed that an inadequate amount of attention was given. Every dad wants to see his daughter supremely loved and so firmly established in the heart of her husband that affection, attention, and consideration are evident.

A second trouble area was that one of the husbands had an apparent lack of solid dependability, which in itself was enough to ruin the marriage. He was one of those guys who just would not buckle down to a productive job but was always "on the verge of making it big." However, success does not come easy. It is one thing to be optimistic; it is another thing to live in a dream world. Maybe you can charge it to immaturity. To describe it accurately, it is a flaw in his character. Too many guys are in the "almost made it big" category. They have the talent, the capacity for achieving material or professional success, yet they never make it because they lack the gumption to struggle and stick to a worthy and productive task.

It all adds up to the fact that it will never be all quiet on the home front if the girl's dad has qualms about the dependability or maturity of the son-in-law. When a guy gets married, it is time for him to be a man and a true husband, so that his wife will know the needed feeling of security.

Look at your marriage through the eyes of her dad. There are some things he is looking for in you. He has a right to expect them of you, because he has given you the dearest thing he has. Having taken a long look, promise the Lord and yourself that you will be that kind of man and husband.

24

Ever So Tenderly

"Ever so tenderly" is a superb heading for a discourse on sex. The act of intercourse is meant to be the most meaningful experience in marriage. It is meant to be filled with beauty and satisfaction, for it is the ultimate expression of the love you have for your wife. Someone has called sex "the servant of love." Beautiful music is the blending of notes in harmony; so lovemaking requires the blending of warmth and tenderness if the beautiful harmony is to be achieved.

Volumes have been written on the subject of sex, and obviously the last word has yet to be written. This I know: each one should enter the tryst with the right feeling or attitude. It is meant to be an act of love, not a means of self-gratification. Each partner needs to understand the other's role. Each should always seek for the other the ultimate in the experience. Remember, it is meant to be a beautiful and enriching act that will deepen your love for each other.

There is another "ever so" that is imperative, namely, "ever so knowingly." On this matter of knowledge, it is my studied conviction that the Church has been silent far too long on the subject of sex education. The neglect can be attributed to the unfounded assumption that sex education is the sole responsibility of the home. Over the years, the leadership of the Church has wanted to believe that parents are competent and knowledgeable instructors and faithful in this essential task. I fear the facts prove otherwise. Unfortunately, the world has not only preempted the parental role of teacher but also has established the standards.

Every Christian young person would do well to listen to what the Word of God has to say on the subject. It is both informative and binding. The Scriptures point wisely to the sacredness of sex. Unmistakably, there is the bold warning about transgression and perversion. God has laid out some keen guidelines, which, if carefully followed, will lead a couple into a beautiful relationship. God created man and woman with sexual faculties and desires. They are to be used and enjoyed; but only when they are correctly used will there be joy. They are meant to convey the magnitude of a couple's love for one another. In the sight of God, the act of love consitutes a sacred union in which oneness is total.

There is no doubt that sex is one of the vital factors in a marriage. Incompatibility here is one of the leading causes for divorce. On the other hand, great sexual success is not the ultimate guarantee of a wonderful marriage.

Though you need not know as much about anatomy and physiology as a doctor, knowledge is imperative. By all means, read a reliable and informative book. Some colossal blunders are due to the fact that one or both partners entered the marriage ignorant of the facts of life. Others have stumbled through the first months of marriage because they assumed they knew all about the birds, the bees, and the wedding bed, when in reality they were woefully ignorant.

Knowledge will go a long way to insure fulfillment in this important aspect of marriage. The knowledge you need covers a variety of facts. To begin with, you need to know the sensitive areas that can be used to stimulate desire and make possible the attainment of the climax every woman needs if she is to enjoy the act wholly. You cannot assume that because your wife is an emotional person, reaching this pinnacle will be quick and easy. Knowledge is not going to guarantee instant success or beautiful fulfillment. It is important for your wife to find the act of love a rewarding experience, and it is your enjoyable task to fashion a satisfying sexual relationship.

You will be greatly helped if you are aware that women are thoroughly and wonderfully romantic. Particularly is this true in sexual activity. They are stimulated by romantic sources that come from a frame of mind, enticing suggestions, and an alluring setting. Anticipation is a great stimulus to a delightful experience. Provocative words and gentle caresses will generate excitement and expectancy. Early in the day you can ignite the embers of eagerness, and the thought will build to incite a flame of desire.

The atmosphere will affect her capacity and interest. To a guy it is "how often," but for the gal it is "how it was done." To her it is the total loving experience and not just the act itself. Someone said, "A man's needs are never more important than a woman's feelings." Words of love can incite desire, and when you follow them with gentle caresses to the sensitive zones, your wife will be aroused. A woman can enjoy the occasion as much as a man, and it is meant to be mutually rewarding.

During the first days or even months of your marriage, you will need to discover what will excite and induce responsiveness. Certainly variety here is the spice of love. The act of love can only be perfected with practice. Initially there will be curiosity and discovery. Accompanying them may be doubts, possibly fears, and even anxieties. One woman put it beautifully, "My husband's thoughtfulness on our wedding night was the key that unlocked the door to our happy marriage."* If there ever is a time for gentleness and tenderness, it is during the honeymoon. Time and perseverance will produce the most satisfying and rewarding experience for both of you. You will want to experiment until there is the greatest possible satisfaction.

*Robert O. Blood Jr., *Marriage* (New York: Free Press, 1969), p. 304.

Naturally no two people are always going to have the same desires at the same time or with the same frequency. One woman's marriage was made for her when her husband said, "I don't ever want sex if you don't share an equal desire to give yourself to it." Don't ever let her lack of desire at that moment fill you with feelings and thoughts that can affect your future acts of love. You won't if you understand your wife's makeup.

There are times when a woman must honestly say, "I'm not in the mood for love." Particularly is this true when her day has been pressure-packed with duties, errands, circle meetings, children, and choir practice. She is totally drained physically and emotionally. She, too, has one thing in mind: a bed. But it is for rest for her weariness and not romance. If you have lovemaking on your mind, forget it! When a wife is exhausted, she cannot be responsive, even if she wants to be. All the charm that a husband possesses and all his wooing wonders will not turn her on. Respect her feelings, and the rewards will be worth the delay.

A woman can get some fulfillment from knowing she has thrilled her husband; yet, on the other hand, nothing builds sexual barriers like the feeling she is being "used." It is far better, far more satisfying, to wait for her total cooperation. The act of love should always be a beautiful and enriching experience that sweetens and solidifies the marriage.

Sex is a supercharged emotional activity that re-

117

quires the giving of each to the other. It is the most intimate relationship, with the greatest revelation of self. There can be no satisfying intercourse if there are marital tensions. Little grievances or hurt feelings simply turn a woman off. They must be dealt with before there can be any thought of sexual activity.

It is terribly important for the wife to know the climactic thrill of orgasm. A woman needs to be stirred by love play. She is slower to be aroused, and it takes her longer to reach a climax. Some men are so erotic that they seek satisfaction only for themselves. A loving husband is always concerned that his wife reach fulfillment so that she, too, can know the thrill of sexual satisfaction. Normally, to bring this about takes practice, patience, and persistence. There is no established rule as to how many attempts it will take before she will be brought to her full glory sexually. Work at it ever so tenderly until she shares the ultimate in love.

Here is a rule worth remembering: no husband should demand more than his wife can give! With all the ingenuity that is yours, surely you can make it exciting and thrilling.

25

A Final Beatitude

A final beatitude for marriage could be "It is more blessed to give than to receive." Even when you transfer this precept from church stewardship to the home, it remains applicable. Actually, giving is needed more in the home than in the church. Another scriptural guideline is in Christ's words that He "came not to be ministered unto, but to minister" (Mark 10:45). For a successful marriage, a man must consider what he can give to the marriage, not just what he will get from it.

Marriage is not self-propelled. If it is to function, it must be energized by the propellants of giving. First of all, seriously and consistently, give your marriage some of your time. This statement may seem naïve, yet the need is basic. Many marriages suffer from pure neglect. With all the demands upon our time in the struggle for survival, and all the duties of the day that keep us on the run, it is imperative that a man keep some time to create *togetherness*. Every marriage must have it. Togetherness is not a feeling only, nor an attitude; it is a time experience.

Prompted by the Lord, I walked into a home one night to talk with a young man whose marriage had lasted a bleak four years. In his evaluation, he said, "I did everything right and according to the book." By this he meant he had married a Christian girl with spiritual background, interests, and convictions. He was convinced that to do so would mean instant success. It could have been great, except that his vocation, plus all his interests and abilities, kept him on a treadmill, but left her lonely, empty, and neglected. It was too late when he realized that he had failed to give time for sharing, for the blending of their lives, and for making their dreams come true.

It is tragic that some men only have time for lovemaking. That is important, but it is not everything. If that is all a couple have going for them, they are in immediate need of a marriage survival kit.

Also, give your marriage some thought. Think seriously about what you want your marriage to be. Goals are as important in marriage as in the business world. Why not accept the wisdom of the business wizards, who declare that men only achieve when they set goals? In your mind, build the structure of your marriage in detail, for then there is the distinct probability of realizing it.

Man is not a victim of environment when it comes to marital planning and fulfillment. I witnessed a marriage that was not flawless, but in a measure, it was beautiful owing to the young man's determination to make it the kind he had missed in his parents' home. Others use their parents' blueprint for their own heaven on earth. Why blunder through in marriage when some planning can make it really wonderful?

So often marriages, like castles in the sand, lose their designed beauty because of thoughtlessness. Apparently many men are so engrossed in their pursuits that the wife's skills and flairs are rarely considered. Every wife deserves an opportunity to give expression to her talents and gifts. It is a wise husband who will provide the opportunity to bring her talents to fruition.

A home can become a dull place if a wife's aesthetic or athletic interests are overlooked. There is an increasing number of couples teaming together on the golf courses and tennis courts, great places for comradeship. One husband I know, although no music buff, faithfully attends operas and concerts with his wife. Much of his enjoyment is derived from watching her obvious ecstacy and knowing the inner delight that music brings to a musical wife.

It doesn't require profound thought to constantly manifest care, cheer, and love. Some might classify them as simple intangibles, yet they are vital. I know of a wife who said to her husband, "It's wonderful just to be with you. You are so much fun and brighten every day." He was the kind of a husband who considerately gave daily to tne marriage and delighted his wife.

One man generously gave to his marriage, which lasted fifty years, the simple things like joy, humor, and kindness. His cheery face, radiant smile, and mischievous eyes could dispel the heaviest gloom. No wonder the marriage was as perfect as possible. Give some thought to what you can do to brighten the way.

If a marriage is going to be rewarding, a man must give of himself. The real significance of the wedding vows is the pledge of giving yourself to your bride and the marriage. I am confident these vows are said in sincerity, but with the demands put on the corporation man or his own concern for his career, the vows often fade or are forgotten. It is difficult for a man to give sufficiently of himself to his marriage when his company, Shylock-like, demands every ounce of his energies and even every drop of his abilities. However, a marriage has a right to its fair share. One partner lamented, "I took everything I could get from my marriage but gave so little." So give yourself unsparingly, as time and circumstances provide the opportunity.

Let me add another biblical truth that is pertinent even when it is applied to marriage: "Give, and it shall be given unto you" (Luke 6:38). Every man, with a minimum of observation, would agree that he has received far more than he has given. It isn't that his wife had done so much more than he. The explanation is that God has taken the "loaves" we have to give and, by His blessing, multiplied them for our good and gain.

No one should attempt to tell you all that you will receive. That would spoil the wonder of it all. It would be like telling you the last chapter of a fictional classic, which would rob you of the challenge and excitement of reading the book. It is equally true that no two marriages are identical and that not everyone receives the same benefits and blessings from his marriage.

An illustrious relative of mine responded to my inquiry about his early enjoyment of marital blessings: "It's not altogether unsatisfactory." That expression became for us a humorous byword for any rewarding marital experience. The years have altered his evaluations, and he has since frequently testified that he, too, has received far more than he has given.

Again, let me emphasize the truth: it is not what you can get from your marriage that is important, but what you can give. By all means, and in every area, give it your best, your very best!

Moody Press, a ministry of the Moody Bible Institute, is designed for education, evangelization and edification. If we may assist you in knowing more about Christ and the Christian life, please write us without obligation to: Moody Press, c/o MLM, Chicago, Illinois 60610.